Transforming Strategy into Success

How to Implement a Lean Management System

Transforming Strategy into Success

How to Implement a
Lean Management System

George A. Shinkle, L.H. "Reb" Gooding, and Michael L. Smith

PRODUCTIVITY PRESS • NEW YORK, NY

Most Productivity Press books are available at quantity discounts when purchased in bulk. For more information contact our Customer Service Department (800-394-6868). Address all other inquiries to:

Productivity Press
444 Park Avenue South, Suite 604
New York, NY 10016
United States of America
Telephone: 212-686-5900
Telefax: 212-686-5411
E-mail: info@productivitypress.com

Composed by William H. Brunson Typography Services
Printed and bound by Malloy Lithographing in the United States of America

Library of Congress Cataloging-in-Publication Data

Shinkle, George A.
    Transforming strategy into success: how to implement a lean management system/George A. Shinkle, L.H. "Reb" Gooding & Michael L. Smith
        p. cm.
Includes bibliographical references and index.
        ISBN 1-56327-299-7
    1. Industrial management—Handbooks, manuals, etc. 2. Leadership—Handbooks, manuals, etc. I. Gooding, L.H. (Lloyd H.) II. Smith, Michael L. III. Title.

HD 31. S455 2004
658.4'012—dc22

                                                            2003024811

07 06 05 04 03   5 4 3 2 1

Dedication

We dedicate this book to all of the people who are striving to improve their organizations through thinking, planning, and then taking action.

May this book offer support in your endeavor and ideas for your success.

TABLE OF CONTENTS

TABLE OF CONTENTS

PREFACE

The intent of this book is to provide insight into how to implement improved strategic intent and lean management systems in organizations. Philosophies, approaches, and technique application are all discussed. The value of embarking on the various parts of the improvement process, as well as cautions about the things that should be avoided, are also covered. Interspersed throughout the book are vignettes, which are intended to illustrate the points being made.

There are a plethora of books on what needs to be done. This book is intended to be a practical guide for executives, managers, supervisors, and future leaders on how to implement strategic intent in a lean manner. It provides proven ideas and concepts from years of business and consulting experience that are applicable to small, medium, and large organizations. It includes perspectives on how to get things done in organizations and how to align organizations to the strategic direction. Chapters 1 through 4 establish the philosophical background and framework for the balance of the book. Chapters 5 through 8 define and discuss Lean Management Systems and strategic direction-setting. Chapters 9 through 12 delve into the complexity of implementation, providing practical methodologies to accomplish real and lasting results. And Chapters 13 and 14 summarize the importance of leadership and establishing Lean Management Systems.

The three key models, which are diagrammed in Chapter 3, are the core of this approach. Those models illustrate these main ideas:

Getting things done. Getting things done is a simple model of what is required to drive organizational progress and get results. It is elegant in its simplicity, yet is extremely difficult to appropriately implement in bureaucratic or heavily political organizations. The entire book revolves around how to get your strategic intent implemented.

Strategic direction-setting. Strategic direction-setting is a focusing activity that aligns the organization's people, assets, teams, and actions on accomplishing desired outcomes through strategic planning and implementation techniques. Its aim is to capture opportunities and deal with chaos in an effective manner. It provides a means for both new and mature organizations to succeed, while dealing with the unique issues that each face. All of the processes outlined in this book are proposed in a way to increase organizational alignment.

Lean Management Systems. The reduction of waste forms the fundamental concept and basis for Lean Management Systems. Lean principles have been very effective in many manufacturing operations; however, they are not limited to the production environment. In fact, enlightened leaders have found that opportunities abound in nonproduction segments of the enterprise. It is intuitively sensible that reducing waste in developing new products and services, getting those products to market faster, selecting the optimum projects in which to invest, improving the supplier network, and reducing roadblocks to peoples' motivation and creativity will yield tremendous dividends.

When all of the processes proposed in this book are linked in an integrated manner, creating a Lean Management System throughout the organization, huge benefits result.

Margin Icons

This book uses small images in the margin to help the reader identify key points.

Identifies sections that will help you achieve your objectives.

Identifies places of particular concern or warnings of possible areas of difficulty.

ACKNOWLEDGEMENTS

This book is an attempt to share our philosophies and techniques on how to make any organization better. It is based on a lifetime of learning from experience in industry and a successful consulting practice. We have touched thousands of people on this journey of learning and have tried not only to help others with our understanding, but also to gain wisdom from those we have touched. We have listed some of the people with whom we have worked who have made a great impact on us. This is not an exhaustive list. The complete list would be too long, and we would inadvertently leave off someone who should be included. To all of you who have helped shape our concepts, provided ideas, offered a place to practice our craft, and have been supportive, we offer our sincere thanks.

Ed Gorman—General Motors
Roger Saillant—Ford
Matthias Rosenbaum—Kolbenschmidt (Germany)
Heinrich Binder—Rheinmetall (Germany)
Yoshihiko Natsume—Toyota
Linda McColgan—NUMMI (New United Motor Manufacturing, Inc.)
Gregory Phillips—Borg Warner
Richard "Dick" Szary—Karl Schmidt Unisia
Eric Diack—DeBeers (AMIC Division) (South Africa)
Peter Carlson—Raychem
Todd Sheppelman—Visteon Corporation
Takehiro Kubo—Toyota
Steve Madinger—Sizzler Corporation
Steve Davis—Visteon Corporation
Bill Ortner—Visteon Corporation
Tom Snyder—Delco Remy America
Rick Stanley—Delco Remy America
Willie Ozbirn—Invensys
Gene Brewer—Invensys
C. Peter Theut—Butzel Long
Marcus Schrenker—Heritage Wealth Management

ACKNOWLEDGEMENTS

Daniel Presslier—Socièté Mosellane de Pistons S. A. (France)
Ike Bayraktar—Aerovironment
Bob Waeiss—Integrity Automotive
Joe Adams—APK
Jim Luckman—Luckman Consulting

Most important of all, to our loving wives, Mary Shinkle and Cindy Gooding, thanks for always being supportive.

Introduction

You have just completed a rolling stop when you look up and see the
flashing lights in your rear-view mirror.
Now the police officer is standing at your window. You say, "What's the
problem officer?"
The police officer says, "You didn't stop at that corner back there."
You say, "Well, I guess I thought I did."
Police officer says, "Well, I guess I thought you didn't!"
You say, "Well, it was my intention to have stopped."
Police officer laughs and says, "Okay, you've caught me in a good mood
and that is a good one. Just be more careful."

This may be one of the few times in life where an excuse is as good as a result.
In the real world, it never is. Only real results count and only real results make
a difference. This is well understood by most people, yet many organizations
work very hard without getting results, without achieving their goals, and in
many cases without getting anything done.

The challenge is to get your good intentions implemented in your organization. Many executives, managers, and supervisors live in frustration as they
struggle to get their teams to accomplish "what is necessary." Many others do
not even recognize how ineffective they really are at getting things done!

How many people want to go home at the end of each day and with pride
tell their families, "I worked very hard all day, achieved none of my goals, and
got nothing done." Yet, many bureaucratic organizations are exactly like
this—finding it exceedingly difficult to accomplish even the simplest of tasks
due to the system and culture that is in place.

Although it may seem acceptable at times, having good intent is not sufficient. This becomes clear when put in a different context. For example, very few people would accept the following examples of so-called good intent: "I intended to be honest on my federal taxes," "I intended to treat people fairly," or "I intended to earn

> *"It is no use saying,*
> *'We are doing our best.'*
> *You have got to succeed in*
> *doing what is necessary."*
>
> Sir Winston S. Churchill—
> British Leader (1874–1965)

my pay." Good intentions alone are just not sufficient! Organizations need to get things done, not just talk about getting them done. One of the choices that organizations need to make is whether they are going to be proactive and decide what they want to be and put in place the required actions, or be reactive and wait until situations present themselves to take any actions remaining open to them. Both choices have ramifications.

A Parable: Hard Working "Firefighters"

There once was an organization with an avowed policy against planning. Their stated strategy was to be completely reactive to every situation that arose. Like the sailboat tacking into the wind, they had committed to follow a zigzag course, from one issue to the next.

This completely reactive approach resulted in an organization that was unfocused at best and counterproductive at worst. They experienced poor efficiency in attempting to accomplish their unstated goals, lost strength as different parts of the organization worked toward competing agendas, and could barely get anything accomplished—even though all the people were working extremely hard.

Competition seemed to get tougher, customers seemed to become more demanding, and technology changes started to occur more often. As the rate of change in the environment multiplied, it became increasingly difficult for the organization to be successful. As the zigzag frequency increased, life in the organization became nearly intolerable as the leaders ricocheted like pinballs from one issue to the next and the workers received either constantly changing direction or no direction at all.

Although they did not understand it at the time, the organization was going through the various phases of reactivity as shown in Figure 1.1. In Phase 1, the issues seemed simple, the appropriate actions seemed clear, and the system even worked well. People who thrived in reactive environments were recruited and given full support and praise for dealing promptly with issues. As long as the supply of able employees was adequate to deal with the number of issues, and the amount of time was adequate to behave this way and not be put out of business by competitors, this system worked. In fact, due to the instant gratification of successfully dealing with problems, this system was somewhat addictive to the successful participants. Those who prospered in it received a regular adrenaline rush. This was called the Fireman Phase since it was like firefighters rushing into burning buildings, rescuing and reviving victims, and dousing the flames. (Start-up organizations often experience this phenomenon.) There was

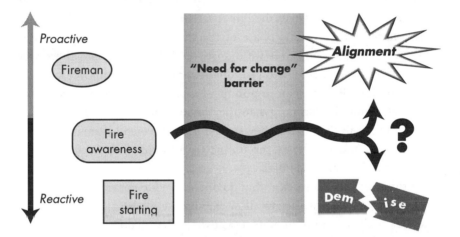

	Phase 1	**Phase 2**	**Phase 3**	**Choice**	
	Fireman	Fire Awareness	Fire Starting	Demise	Alignment
# Fires	= # Firefighters	> # Firefighters	>>> # Firefighters	More & bigger	Being reduced
Strategy on fires	Love them	Reduce # of them	Start them	Watch them	Resolve them
Firefighters	Rewarded	Frustrated	Blamed	Quit	Focused
Morale	High	Declining	Everyone for themselves	Negative	Increasing
Teams	Aligned	Misalignment encroaching	Rampant misalignment	Absent	Aligned
Organization	Static	Repeated reorganization	Chaos	Confusing	Flexible & clear

Figure 1.1: Stages of Reactiveness

often a frenzy of activity in reacting to situations. It was the positive energy associated with this phase that was attractive to many employees. However, this became very expensive, since the supply of able employees had to be continually increased to deal with the mounting number of issues.

In Phase 2, the organization could no longer afford the number of people required to react to all of the issues and, in essence, fires went unattended and buildings burned to the ground. Morale dropped as the instant gratification of Phase I became instant condemnation for jobs not being done. (This often is experienced when start-ups grow too fast or when mature organizations experience cutbacks.) The positive energy of Phase I was transformed to a negative force. The organization was blamed and the agreed fix was to reorganize. This became known as the Fire Awareness Phase.

In Phase 3, the terminal phase of reactivity, the organization became paralyzed. Since so many fires were unsuccessfully fought and there were negative rewards for being involved, the previously able employees avoided fighting the fires. Rather than responding to issues as required, they created issues that required attention when they knew that they could successfully deal with them. In this phase, they started fires, dragged victims into burning buildings, and waited by the phone to respond to the call. This was known as the Fire Starting Phase.

At this point it became clear that no one wanted to continue working this way. The choice was whether to allow the demise of the organization or to make drastic changes to resuscitate it. Knowing what to do to solve a problem is necessary, but alone it is not sufficient to resuscitate an organization such as the one in the parable. Knowing how to do what needs to be done is critical. The people in the parable, just as in real life, have the opportunity to take the necessary actions. This book is written for those who choose the path toward strategic alignment and success and are looking for methods and approaches to avoid becoming like the parable.

Business Systems and Strategic Intent

Successful strategic implementers recognize the impact of the environmental system on their situation, the complexity of the organizational system in which they operate, and that choosing a direction is not for the faint of heart. In business organizations the system, in simplest terms, consists of people, strategy, structure, and process, as graphically depicted in Figure 1.2.

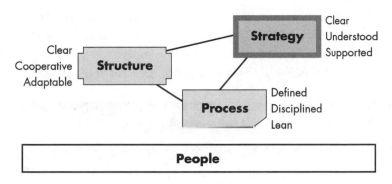

Figure 1.2: Business Systems Perspective

People, strategy, structure, and process sound simple. However, the system is very dynamic with many elements such as time, competition, customers, politics, organizational culture, and personalities. It also is interactive, and actions taken can change the playing field and its dynamics, as in every system. Making organizational change is difficult; however:

- The system can be changed.
- Progress can be made.
- Paradoxes and paradigms will challenge the change agents.
- Thinking will always be required—sometimes the thinking will be counterintuitive.
- The risk of unintended consequences exists.
- The only way to get something done is to get started, learn, and adapt accordingly.

Many organizations are making significant improvements in every aspect of how they conduct their business, as they simultaneously adapt to an ever-changing world. The challenge is how to learn from these organizations and their experiences. Organizations that are successfully growing seem to somehow select the best opportunities and capture them. They seem to be able to accomplish the impossible and are having fun doing it. While cost cutting and downsizing have been the primary focus of many mature organizations, some are beginning to recognize that these approaches alone do not necessarily provide the long-term desired results. They may improve the short-term survival prognosis, but often the fundamental strength of the organization is undermined. So the dilemma is how to retain the things that made the organization successful while streamlining and refocusing it. For new and growing enterprises, the challenge is to choose the right opportunity at the right time, which is aligned with the skills and abilities of the organization. Whether new or mature, successful organizations realize that they should incorporate a systematic approach, not simply to get things done in a general sense—but to get the right things done at the right times.

IN THE REAL WORLD...

On rare occasions in our industry and consulting experience, we have had the opportunity to work with teams whose performance was truly exceptional with respect to implementing strategic intent. We have labeled these groups as superperforming teams (SPTs). In each case these superteams shared a set of characteristics that were not totally present in ordinary groups.

One of the more surprising characteristics about these exceptional teams was that they were not composed of exceptional people. They had a core of very good performers, but they were not a collection of all-stars. They were typically average (and sometimes below average) in their skills and abilities.

They always had a very clear understanding of their vision of the future and of what they intended to accomplish. In each case, this vision was very different from the current state, and it was a tremendous stretch to be able to reach it (e.g., grow from nearly zero market share to an industry dominant position in four years). Each member of the SPT could articulate the vision and wanted to support it.

The SPTs had strong top leaders who constantly supported and encouraged them to accomplish the shared vision. They also had strong midlevel leaders within the organization. All leaders practiced an approach of inclusion and encouraged all team members to take on as much as they could. No one was denied the opportunity to pursue activities beyond their experience.

The SPTs believed that they were part of a noble cause and were willing to make personal sacrifices for that cause. In one case, the SPT was a small unit within a large organization. The SPT believed that part of their cause was to save the parent organization and create a new model, which would be copied by the balance of the organization. There was an attitude of "we are part of something, and we must all support each other to accomplish our vision."

Getting these things done requires focusing on:

1. Deciding what you want to do (i.e., vision, mission, and objectives).
2. Providing targets (i.e., metrics and goals).
3. Assuring values are understood.

Each of the SPTs not only had a vision for the future, but they also had very tangible strategies for achieving it. Most were very focused on either satisfying a particular customer, or on defeating a specific competitor. All of the team members knew exactly who the key customer or competitor was. They could also clearly relate how their actions would impact the customer or competitor. They regularly took stock of where they were, evaluated what was working and what was not working, and reformed their strategies appropriately. They had strong implementation and follow-up systems and knew where they were in relation to their plan. While they had a well-understood plan, they were not overly attached to it. They were willing to modify the plan when their follow-up system indicated that what they were doing was not yielding the desired results. They knew specifically how to define success (and failure), and worked tirelessly to achieve what they set out to do.

The best superperforming teams had a no-blaming approach to interpersonal relations. The attitude was "we win or lose as a team, and we do what is needed to accomplish the tasks at hand." There was a strong willingness to pitch in and help team members accomplish what needed to be done, whether it was part of the individual's job description or not.

As a result of all of these characteristics, the level of camaraderie was very high. These teams often worked very long hours to accomplish their goals. In spite of the long hours, they would often find reasons to associate socially outside of the work environment. There seemed to be a special chemistry present in these teams.

We hope that each of you gets at least one opportunity to be a part of a superperforming team sometime during your life. Everyone who does says it was one of the most rewarding experiences of his or her life.

We have integrated our learning from these SPTs into the processes suggested throughout this book.

4. Providing methods (i.e., processes) to accomplish the goals.
5. Always working to get better.

The successful approach discussed in this book is based on strategic systems thinking, people involvement, strategic planning, teamwork, reengineering, lean systems, problem solving, and implementation management techniques, all integrated to provide the desired results. The challenge is how to implement good strategic intentions, with an energized, motivated, and creative team.

Much has been written on the subject of command and control versus empowerment models for running organizations. The command and control model emanates from military dogma. It has a well-defined hierarchy, strict lines of communication, and a concept of giving and following orders. This model is aimed at efficiently creating and spreading intended actions throughout the entire organization. It requires not only that the intended actions be created at the top levels but also that a strict control scheme is in place to ensure that the actions are implemented. This correctly suggests that the implementers can be motivated, forced, or coerced to follow the orders.

The empowerment model, on the other hand, is based on the premise that by accessing the good ideas of everyone, better solutions will be created and that those who are given the opportunity to participate in the process of creating the intended actions are more likely to willingly implement them. It is aimed at effectiveness in creating and implementing superior solutions. This method is often inefficient in the time it takes to decide on intended actions; however, it often yields more creative actions and requires less motivating, forcing, or coercing to ensure that the actions are implemented. Simply stated, the command and control model requires the person at the top of the hierarchy always to know the right thing to do, while the empowerment model requires participation from large portions of the organization to draw out creativity and energize implementation.

Neither of these models is right for all situations. In large, complex, multifaceted organizations that exist in dynamic environments, it is difficult, if not impossible, for the person at the top of the hierarchy to have enough knowledge always to know the right thing to do. Even in these organizations, there are situations that demand quick efficiency in creating and implementing the actions; thus, time does not allow for the empowerment model to "bubble up" an answer. The most effective organizations have found an appropriate balance between the two extremes and effortlessly move back and forth between the models, depending on the situation.

A Personal Note from the Authors

If there is only one thing that you remember as you read this book on how to get things done, it is the following philosophy:

The cornerstones of getting things done

- Start at the end.
- Keep it simple.
- Think it through to the end.

Start at the end. The key to getting things done is to know where you are going and to focus on what you want to accomplish. Many make the mistake of spending most of their time analyzing thoroughly where they are, rather than focusing on where they want to be. By starting at the end as you evaluate the options facing you in any situation, you become more focused on the desired outcome and less distracted by the noise associated with what is happening in the present. This does not mean that you should ignore the present. It will be crucial to understand your current position as you chart a new course—it will determine the degrees of freedom that you have. Just do not let it distract or mislead you from the desired result.

Keep it simple. The best approaches are almost always the simplest ones. Less experienced people often rely too much on analysis. This reliance is usually based on a belief that detailed analysis of current data will make the decision straightforward. Always ask what you will do with the information once you have finished analyzing and processing it. Avoid complex overanalysis. Many organizations waste significant resources on complex analysis techniques that are not consistent with the real decision processes that will be used. (We could tell many stories here — but you probably already have some of your own.) A useful rule of thumb is that if more analysis will not help you get to where you are going, do not do it! Sometimes a complex plan as a result of a detailed analysis is required, but usually the simplest plan is better.

Think it through to the end. Always check for consistency. Will the chosen approach work in your organization's situation? Have you considered all the details? What will your competitors do? Will your customers accept your approach? Does your organization have the capabilities and competence to implement the chosen path? The most dangerous approach is the one that is *almost* right. Like a second-best poker hand (where you bet as though you will win, but you never do), it will be the most costly approach in the end. A common error is to assume away those little details that make it difficult to accomplish what you want to do. Remember, if it were not for gravity, every-one could fly. By thinking it through to the end, you can expose and deal with the inconsistencies that may undermine the success of your approach.

Summary

The philosophy of this book is that the secret to implementing strategic intent is to involve as many of the appropriate people as is feasible to gain access to ideas, and to energize them to implement the chosen path. The goal should always be to maintain an appropriate balance between efficiency and effec-tiveness. Either one taken to extremes will not lead to desired results. Never underestimate the potential of motivated people to accomplish more than is thought to be possible.

In the Beginning
It Is Leadership

Leadership is the magic key to successful
implementation of strategic intent.

Leadership exists at all levels of an organization and is the key ingredient to getting things done. Leading an organization is much easier from the top of the hierarchy. However, leaders at all levels are instrumental in accomplishing organizational desires. Organizations that lack depth of leadership almost always seem to struggle to be successful as compared to those where leadership has been cultivated, nurtured, and carefully developed throughout the entire organization. Figure 2.1 shows a model of leadership with values, business competence, technical (or functional) competence, and people competence as the key aspects, with a base of energy, courage, and responsibility. Leaders should be focused on implementing strategic intent. Energy is required to push, and push, and push against what will be significant organizational resistance to any change. Courage is needed to define difficult and sometimes unpopular direction, and to do what is necessary. A sense of responsibility and stewardship for the legacy that the leaders are protecting is a fundamental requirement. Leaders communicate (or create) the need to change, and they apply the continuous pressure to drive ongoing progress to accomplish the strategic intent of the organization.

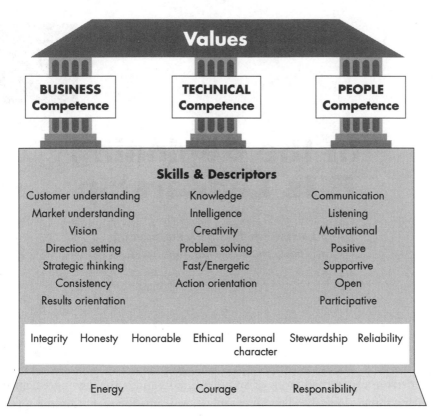

Figure 2.1: Model of Leadership

It is the leader's responsibility to define the strategic intent of the organization. Or more precisely stated, it is the leader's responsibility to have a strategic intent for the organization and to ensure that it is implemented. Some top managers struggle in defining the strategic intent for the organization, and that is manageable as long as they recognize it. Every organization requires a well-conceived strategic intent, and if top managers are not capable of defining it, they must seek assistance in creating and implementing it. (Team approaches to planning and implementation are discussed in Chapter 4, and strategic direction setting is discussed in Chapter 7.)

High Expectations

Leaders get what they expect. Leaders must expect high performance and they must expect disciplined adherence to the processes of the organization.

Target 1: Aim high to achieve more than you think is possible. Organizations and people are exactly the way they want to be. If they want to change, they do. Leaders should set high expectations, but be reasonable in how people are treated when they fall short of meeting those expectations. Effective leaders are adept at challenging people to strive to accomplish the impossible, without giving up because the task seems too difficult. They also must be able to identify who is capable, who is not, and to place people where they will be likely to succeed. They must also identify and move those people who are blocking the success of the organization.

Target 2: Disciplined adherence, not blind obedience. Organizations with disciplined processes make progress faster than organizations without structured approaches. Discipline has become a bad word in many corporate cultures. Every organization needs its employees to be creative and motivated and simultaneously disciplined in their adherence to the process requirements. This is not a dichotomy—it just requires knowledge and understanding of what is required and where creativity is desired (or allowed). Blind adherence leads to lackluster performance and horrible motivation levels. It can also evolve into malicious obedience—that is, employees doing only what they are told—*exactly*, regardless of the consequences. A balance must be maintained where the environment is flexible enough to allow creative innovation while structured enough to ensure that the creative ideas are implemented efficiently.

Process or Results?

Many ask where management should focus—on processes or on results? The answer is both. Of course, every organization must produce results. If the organization does not produce the results expected by the stakeholders, it eventually will cease to exist. It is the role of the leaders of the organization to decide which processes increase the likelihood of achieving the desired results. Focusing on results without processes is like trying to drive a car by stepping on the accelerator pedal, but without touching the steering wheel. Leaders must do both.

Invest in Strategy

Many organizations believe that knowing all the information will somehow make the answer automatically visible. This may indeed be true; however, investing the money and time needed to collect all the possible information regarding any particular issue is not a practical solution for today's organizations, and, in many cases, all of the information will never be available. Yet, many organizations spend 95 percent of their energy and resources in collecting data, and then have only 5 percent left to invest in determining what it means and what to do about it. This is called understrategizing. Caution should be exercised to avoid both overanalyzing and understrategizing.

Many management books suggest: "just do something—anything." This sounds absolutely ridiculous to some. However, since these proponents have seen a paralysis in the management ranks of many organizations, this do any-

IN THE REAL WORLD...

Several years ago, while working with a troubled organization, we noticed that they had a very high propensity to analyze everything to great depths. At first, this seemed commendable because they had a significant amount of data to assist them in making decisions. However, we soon noticed that rather than using the data to actually make decisions, they were using their lack of data (claiming to never have enough) to avoid making decisions. For example, they would spend a significant amount of time analyzing their cost structure on a troubled product line and comparing it to their competitors' cost structure. They seemed to be more concerned whether they were 11.3 percent or 11.4 percent worse than their competition, when their concern simply should have been that they were significantly behind their competition. As a first step, we had them reassign half of the resources that would have normally been used to analyze the numbers. They were assigned to address the gap and to develop an action plan that could be implemented. We discovered this analysis-driven behavior was rooted deep in the culture of the organization. In less than four months, when the action plan development team reported to management their recommendations, management asked for more data. At this point we chose to intercede by asking specifically, "What data is needed in order to make a decision?" After carefully documenting all of management's data requirements, we asked, "When you have all this data, will you be able to make a decision?"

thing suggestion makes perfect sense as a way to get movement started. The risk of this mentality is that the data that does exist will be ignored. Obviously there must be checks and balances to ensure that the actions that are implemented are appropriate. A prejudice toward action over inaction is suggested.

Throughout this book it is strongly suggested that organizations spend more time on strategy and implementation than on analysis. A big part of change leadership is tackling the difficult but critical things that must be done to make progress. Critical issues cannot be ignored just because they look hard. Most organizations understand their situation and are just avoiding taking the necessary action simply because it may be difficult or distasteful.

> After some contemplation, management agreed that they would be able to decide on a course of action with this data. We considered their data requirements and realized that each of their questions could be answered directionally with about four hours of work. We told the management group, "It appears that we could answer these questions by the end of the day. Let's meet at 5:00 PM and make a decision!" As you can imagine, there were some shocked looks on the faces of the management team. They agreed to meet, but it was apparent that they did not believe that their data requirements would be met. We showed the action planning team how to answer each of the questions with directional data. At 5:00 PM we reconvened and addressed each of the issues. At the end of the discussion the management group, somewhat incredulously, said I guess we don't have any choice but to make a decision.
>
> **The moral:** Get on with doing what needs to be done. Ensure your data requirements are adding value. Many parts of strategic management require data *accuracy*, but not data *precision*.
>
> **Management hint:** In our consulting experience on significant company or organizational issues, approximately 20 percent have required precise data analysis to resolve, while the remaining 80 percent were solved with macrolevel data investigation.

Invest in Systems Analysis and Systems Thinking

Leaders who are attempting to make significant change should consider the complex interactions of the organizational system—that is, the people, politics, culture, motivations, adaptability, level of empowerment, level of process discipline, clarity of direction, leadership strength, anxiety level, level of rebelliousness, history of the organization, level of reality, strength of commitment, and so on. Many leaders have been frustrated by organizations that do not seem to respond logically. (This means the reactions to inputs were not what was expected or predicted.)

Organizational systems are sometimes complex, paradoxical, counterintuitive, and unpredictable. Leaders and change agents must consider how the processes do work in the organization, how the interactions operate, what motivates the system, and what just annoys the system. This book proposes several aspects of systems pressurization for leaders, including significant people involvement, public visual initiative management, and a process focus balanced by results requirements.

Leaders must carefully consider all proposed changes in light of the understanding of the organizational system that exists at the time and think them through, considering likely outcomes and possible side effects. The successful systems thinkers learn to use the organizational culture—much like an expert of judo uses the weight of his opponent as leverage—taking advantage of the organizational system dynamics to accomplish the desired change.

Leadership Balance

Like most things in management, the answer to how to lead effectively is balance, and strategically choosing appropriately for the specific situation. The leadership balance graphic in Figure 2.2 shows that leaders must make situation-specific decisions every minute of every day. They must choose which side of the balance on which to stand during each encounter. The balance point is completely dependent on the culture of their organization. There is no single answer to where the balance point will be for each of these issues.

The Leadership Ego Challenge

The very first requirement of effective leadership is for leaders to understand that others in the organization may know things that they do not. Stated more

Figure 2.2: The Leadership Balance

directly, leaders must first accept that they are not necessarily the smartest people in the world (or the only smart people in the world). Once this is accomplished, the value of getting other people involved in setting direction and planning implementation becomes clear.

Leaders who truly value the people in their organization have made the first giant step toward implementing their strategic intent. "How" begins with leadership that values the people, respects their perspectives, and dignifies their presence in the organization. True leaders find the best way to become facilitators for their organization, much like the conductor of an orchestra who depends on the talent of the musicians in order to create beautiful music.

Summary

In observing organizations around the world, every successful strategic implementation, every successful change implementation, and every successful management system implementation had one thing in common—a strong, capable leader in a position to drive and maintain progress. Leaders of all types can be successful—but leadership of some kind is required.

The Business
System Models

All models are wrong.
Some models are useful.

Dr. George E.P. Box, Professor
and Quality Expert—1979

Traditionally, models are used to help understand or explain complexity in more simple terms. When modeling a complex situation, often some of the details that create the complexity are lost in the simplification of the model. Therefore, models are usually not completely accurate, yet they have proven to be very helpful. The three foundational models for this book are:

- The getting things done model
- The business planning and direction setting model
- The management system brick wall model

The getting things done model. The getting things done model is shown in Figure 3.1. The fundamental factors that drive successful implementation of strategic intent are: leadership, direction, principles, metrics (goals), processes, and an improvement methodology.

As previously stated, it all starts with leadership. In the absence of effective leadership, organizations just do not get the right things done. For leadership to be effective, appropriate direction must be set. The direction must be understood, accepted, and embraced by a critical mass of the organization. It is not good enough for the leader to say, "We're going east," if the critical

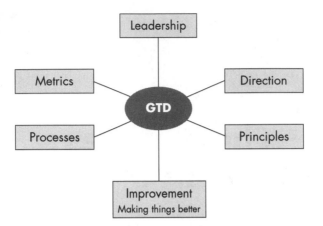

Figure 3.1: Getting Things Done Model

mass says, "Okay, have a good trip. We'll see you when you get back." Common processes that effectively support implementation of the direction are required. Success comes from following the processes that repeatedly lead to getting the results that are expected and desired. Appropriate metrics help facilitate implementation. Metrics must fit the required cadence of the organization, telling everyone what needs to be done and when. Without metrics, organizations will depend on luck to implement the right things at the right time. This all must be supported by the guiding principles. No matter how well anything is implemented, it can always be improved. The most successful organizations are constantly looking for ways to improve their business.

The business planning and direction-setting model. The business planning and direction-setting model is shown in Figure 3.2. Before we can implement our good intentions, we must define those good intentions. This model is about planning—the art of capturing our good intentions.

The first thing to note about the business planning and direction-setting model is that it is not linear—it is circular and interactive. It is much easier to think that one should first set the strategic direction and then sequentially put in place all the other supporting plans and activities to ensure that strategic intent is followed. Unfortunately, the world does not seem to work that way due to the interactive effects of the other plans and activities on the strategic direction. The circular nature of the model shown in Figure 3.2 is based on an epiphany reached from dealing with well-meaning people

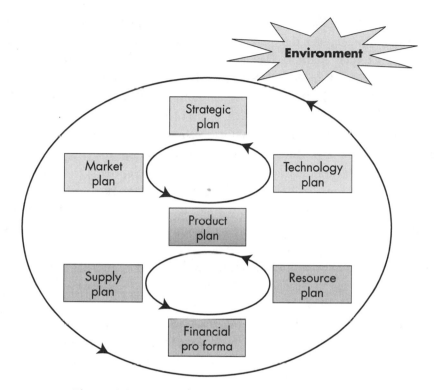

Figure 3.2: Business Planning and Direction-Setting Model

with different points of view. In a marketing-oriented organization, people say, "Everyone knows that to be market-driven, the market plan must drive the strategic plan." In a technology-oriented organization, people say, "Everyone knows that to be technology-driven, the technology plan must drive the strategic plan." In a strategically-oriented organization, people say, "Everyone knows that the strategic plan must drive all subsequent plans." Actually, because the market, technology, and strategic plans are so interdependent, it hardly matters which one is done first. What does matter is that all three are allowed to interact until the appropriate and consistent strategic direction is reached in each.

The strategic plan, the market plan, the technology plan, and the product (or services) plan all interact. The feedback based on the direction that is set in any of these plans impacts the possible actions of all the other plans. For example, if the market plan says we should pursue customer X, it may drive the technology plan to work on those technologies that will best fit the needs of customer X. On the other hand, if the technology plan specifies that we will develop technology 23, the market plan may specify that, in that case, we can pursue customers A and B. Having this new technology 23 and being able to pursue customer B may be sufficient to alter or augment the strategic direction. In other words, these plans interact and percolate until they are frozen for implementation. It is best to start with a planned strategic direction as the framework for developing the market, technology, and product plans, but then look for opportunities to improve the overall approach, based on the insight derived from the interaction during this development.

After the strategic direction and its associated market and technology plans have been frozen, the product plan can also be frozen. The product plan serves as the impetus for developing the appropriate plans for how the product will be supplied to the market, what resources and skills will be required, and what the financial impact will be. If the financial pro forma is insufficient to meet the needs of the organization, iteration in either loop may be required.

A critical element that many organizations often ignore is time. It is the one resource that can never be regained once it has been squandered. Yet it is often treated as if it is infinite, and that the impact of squandering it is negligible. In creating the appropriate strategic direction for an organization, it is critical to start early. In creating a robust marketing strategy, it is often necessary to embark on a chosen path prior to knowing the real customer needs or the true market demand. Invention takes time and is often costly. Starting on the technology path at the appropriate time often determines whether the organization will be successful or not. Rarely does procrastination improve the strategy of an organization. The secret to having more time is to start earlier. Time may actually be the most precious resource any organization has.

> *Just because we cannot see clearly the end of the road, that is no reason for not setting out on the essential journey. On the contrary, great change dominates the world, and unless we move with the change we will become its victims.*
>
> Robert F. Kennedy—U.S. Senator and Presidential Candidate (1925–1968)

The management system brick wall model. There are many components to any management system. For a management system to operate effectively, the components need to be organized like a set of building blocks in a brick wall.

Such a management system brick wall model is shown in Figure 3.3. While there are many bricks in the wall of any management system, the people and the organizational culture, which creates the foundation, are the critical parts. This management system model is based on many of the concepts of the Toyota Production System and lean methods. The Toyota Production System and lean methodologies are well documented in numerous other books and will not be reiterated here.

The building blocks or bricks in the wall are intended to represent the major processes, tools, or practices that cause an organization to work. In almost any organization, any of these building blocks can be improved to make the organization work better. Selecting which building blocks would be the best to improve, from a priority standpoint, requires a detailed analysis of the specific situation. Each of the building blocks is important, but some may provide more value in a specific situation or organization. Thoughtful analysis of the situation, combined with an understanding of the potential benefits of the lean building blocks, typically yields a clear direction. A common mistake is to randomly choose which building blocks to improve in an unconnected fashion.

All the bricks are important; however, the cornerstone bricks of customer relations and documented processes are crucial in any management system. Improvement in the management system is built from the bottom up. Foundation building requires that people understand and accept their responsibilities, that a robust communication methodology exists, and that there is strong tactical management. The direction-setting row of bricks (previously discussed in Figure 3.2) is aimed at defining what is and what is not desired, as well as achieving organizational alignment. Without the direction-setting, people within organizations often inadvertently work on the wrong things. Once the first two rows of bricks are in place, work can begin on creating the lean structure and improving the lean operation. Information flow is critical to ensure that intended actions are being implemented. Communications must be optimized, an appropriate meeting structure and schedule must be established, and choosing an appropriate methodology for reviewing key metrics should be determined. The management system must ensure that a quality system is embedded throughout the organization and that the appropriate tools and practices are in place. The top row of bricks is business leadership. It must ensure that all the pieces are in place and that the necessary skills and competencies are present. It must focus on goal attainment, support of

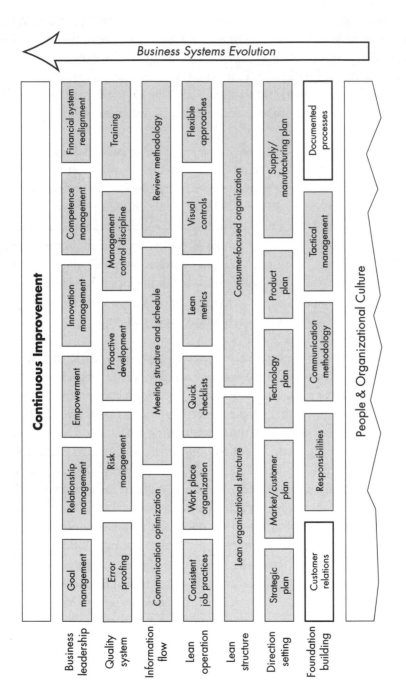

Figure 3.3: The Management System Brick Wall Model

innovation, empowerment, and ensuring that relationships among people and organizations are healthy. The capstone to the wall is continuous improvement. The strongest organizations are never satisfied with how well they conduct their business. They are always looking for ways to make it better.

Summary

These three models have successfully been used to transform many organizations of all sizes. The remainder of this book further details how to implement these concepts to achieve the desired results.

Organizations are exactly the way they want to be...

If an organization wants to be different, it changes. To achieve any organizational transformation, therefore, one must first change what the organization wants to be. How does one get the organization to want what they should be wanting? This is discussed in detail in the next chapter.

4

The Magic Is in the How—
Not in the What

Most people know what needs to be done;
the challenge is how to get it done.

Most management books deal with the subject of *what* needs to be done to improve the business; fewer deal with exactly *how* to do this. This is because the *what* can be more generally applied to any organization. However, the how depends on the specifics of the individual organizational culture, its leadership, the problems being faced, and the people and personalities involved. Furthermore, the how is always an integrated set of activities that must be carried out in parallel, which is difficult to describe linearly (as books are written). In the following chapters the integrated activities are disassembled, evaluated, discussed, and then reassembled. The following pieces, which make *how* possible are examined: lean management systems, guiding principles, strategic direction, metrics and goals, process structure, discipline and relentless follow-up, technique selection and application, and improvement mentality. To gain maximum benefit, the methods and hints discussed throughout these chapters should be considered in context with the organizational "system" and applied as a total management system approach.

Before delving into each of these areas in depth, a philosophical overview may be helpful. While each situation is unique, there are some general approaches that have proven to be successful in a multitude of situations. More than half of organizational improvement activities are less successful than intended. Since these activities usually take tremendous effort, one must ask why the success rate is so low. There are many reasons, but a common observation is that, in such cases, no clear vision of the desired change existed and the organization was not appropriately engaged to create the improvement. To quote a German client: "Around here we have autocratic decision making with democratic implementation! Management yells the decisions and orders and we decide which ones to do!"

The irony of the situation is that the person quoted was a member of management. So if barking orders does not lead to motivated implementation, what is the appropriate approach? How do you get an organization to want what it should want? Though there is no formula to answer this question, some elements must always be present. There must always be a clearly articulated vision of what is wanted. Alignment to support implementation of the vision must always be created. The people in the organization must always be fully engaged in the vision to participate in creating the necessary changes, and they must be given a clear reason to change. If any of these elements are missing, successful change will not take place. Whatever is being improved, always decide what needs to be done first, then determine how to try to accomplish what is needed. Involve as many people as is practical, both in determining what is needed and in determining how it will be accomplished. The value of involving many people is that it makes implementation much easier. The danger of involving many people is that it is a much slower process and the content may be diluted. One must always be on guard to ensure that content is not compromised and that progress is not significantly delayed in order to have broad involvement.

So now the focus must be on how to accomplish these aims. Including those we have mentioned above, here are the core elements:

1. Have a vision.
2. Build support (alignment).
3. Engage people.
4. Learn to work by working.
5. Take away fear.
6. Instill and improve.

Having a Vision Is Critical

The vision should define what the organization intends to be in the future. The vision is not intended to be a motto. It must be created in sufficient detail

> *Set the case you want to build a boat.*
> *Rather than pushing people to buy*
> *wood and to get tools and rather*
> *than giving work assignments you*
> *should teach the people the desire*
> *for the wide, endless ocean.*
>
> Antoine de Saint-Exupery—
> French Novelist and Aviator (1900–1944)

so that the future can be fully visualized and embraced. At the same time, it must be general enough so that it does not prescribe a strict adherence to a specific set of actions. It must be flexible enough to allow for creativity and future improvement. A common misjudgment is to view the vision as a fluffy slogan. Many want to skip this step and move on to the more robust processes of setting challenging objectives and goals for the organization. However, the key step in creating organizational alignment is to create a vision of an inviting future and a clear reason to change from the current state. It is difficult to engage people in meeting the goals of increased revenue and decreased mistakes when they do not understand how this fits into the future vision, as the Saint-Exupery quotation highlights.

The Magic Solution Is Alignment

It is truly rare to observe an organization that knows exactly what it wants to be and how it intends to achieve what it wants. Even when organizations do have a clear vision of their intended future, it is often not sufficient to ensure that the vision will be met. The leaders must find a way to build the dedicated support of the entire team. The magic of getting things done is in how the leader goes about building the team's understanding, support, and commitment to action.

Since no one can corner the market on good ideas, finding ways to identify and implement the best ideas is a common characteristic of successful organizations. Making sure that everyone in the organization supports the direction and is motivated to implement the best ideas requires having a perfectly aligned organization. Many organizations decide that this takes too much time, do not do the necessary things to create alignment, and then they become unhappy with their low performance.

When properly designed, any improvement activity can be carried out in a way that increases organizational alignment. Of course, there is no magic formula that will solve all the problems and remove all the misalignment in every

> *The best ideas without*
> *implementation are worthless!*

Organizational alignment does require an investment of time, but when properly done, its payoff is tremendous. Focusing on effectiveness rather than efficiency is critical when the intent is to align people around achieving a set of goals and on moving in a new direction.

organization. Organizational alignment is a concept that must be tailored to individual organizations to match their business, philosophy, culture, and specific situation. Tailoring is required to ensure that the improved direction and systems can and will be implemented.

Achieving alignment is a real challenge for many organizations. It requires time to discover, discuss, and understand key issues and different perspectives. While achieving alignment requires broad participation within the organization, everyone cannot be involved in everything unless the organization is very, very small. An effective alternative is to use small groups to delve into the details and to communicate the conclusions to the larger population. Allowing for additional feedback on critical items is often beneficial.

IN THE REAL WORLD

It is easy to see the benefits of aligning a large organization; however, even small organizations can benefit tremendously. A successful entrepreneur with whom we were working once told us that he had mentally resolved everything and nothing more needed to be done to define the company direction and operating principles. We agreed that he certainly must have resolved everything to create his successful company, but we asked him to please humor us and allow us to document his thinking so that we could understand what is happening and be better prepared to help him. After several hours of discussion and writing the results on chart paper, the whole story could be visualized, and it became clear to the entrepreneur that he was giving conflicting directions that were holding back the entire company. Deciding on a direction, writing it down, and sharing it with his employees allowed him to resolve many conflicts. Once the entrepreneur implemented a strategic action follow-up system, he became less frustrated, had more time for business and personal development, and was much more successful. In addition, the people who worked for him were happier.

People Must Be Engaged

The leadership challenge is to create an organization that captures opportunity, that gets the best ideas from its people, and that gets support and commitment for implementation of those ideas. In other words, leadership must create an organization that captures the creativity and motivation of all the people in it to accomplish the strategic direction. Success does not automatically follow from having a vision and an aligned organization. Nothing happens unless action is taken, so it is critical to energize the people to take steps to implement the appropriate actions. A vision without actions is just a wish, and it is actions, not wishes, that turn a vision into a reality. When these actions are identified, an approach to ver-

> *You cannot teach a man anything. You can only help him discover it within himself.*
>
> Galileo Galilei—Italian Astronomer and Physicist (1564–1642)

ify that each has been implemented properly is critical to achieving the desired result. In Chapter 10, where discipline and follow-up are reviewed, a method for creating those actions and organizing them into a set of initiatives with an implementation system is discussed. The most successful organizations engage the people at all levels of the organization to take the actions that are required.

Learn to Work by Working

A key benefit of broad involvement in improvement activities is that it creates the opportunity to train many people to be better prepared to run the business, or to make major contributions to it. Learning and understanding always seem to be better ingrained in people when the activity in which they are engaged can be directly applied to their work. In other words, people learn to work by working. This phenomenon has been observed in organizations of all sizes and in locations all over the world.

The concept of experiential learning in implementing strategic intent is to involve people in actually assessing, designing, and implementing the strategic and lean improvements into the organization. One of the major concepts of the lean implementation approach is to make the *best* way, the way work is done. To further the sustainability of the strategy, make the way work gets done consistent with the new strategy and new process philosophies. Allowing everyone to learn the new way by doing it in their specific area of responsibility builds internalized understanding and the ability to repeat the process unassisted, thereby building sustainability.

Take Away Fear

People are unlikely to engage in activities that move very far outside of the borders of the status quo when they are afraid. Organizations that are intent on making significant improvements must create an environment where fear of making mistakes does not paralyze the organization. Of course, there must be accountability. No one wants everyone in the organization to freely go around making mistakes in everything they do. The best organizations adroitly balance the seemingly mutually exclusive conditions of freedom from fear (destructive fear and anxiety) and personal accountability.

At low and moderate levels fear can be motivational and spark creativity while at high levels fear can become destructive and create anxiety. The majority of the destructive fear within organizations is caused by management. Openness and trust are definite benefits when transitioning to a model of involvement. Management must make it acceptable to speak openly and present differing views. Management of organizations can nurture openness or, on the other hand, easily (and sometimes unintentionally) kill it. There are many resources on leadership philosophy and participative management, so these topics will not be addressed in detail here.

When the fear of job loss is associated with an organizational improvement activity, the likelihood of successful implementation will be reduced due to lack of support from the people who must implement the improvement. Hence the removal of this fear, whether real or imaginary, is critical to success. It is problematic to ask people to eliminate their own jobs or, for that matter, to eliminate their particular job assignment. Management credibility is critical so honesty is highly suggested. Because lean improvement activities are meant not only to reduce costs but to free up time or resources to complete additional activities and to take on new customers and programs, the organization can typically make an honest pledge to redeploy people whose jobs are no longer needed due to the improvement activity. People will then be more likely to support the activity, and this is the optimum position. In difficult situations, where employment must be reduced, improvement is the best way to increase the probability of an ongoing organization and the future ability to rehire people that might need to be furloughed in the short term. The fear of job loss should be addressed as a part of the initial lean project activity and a clear position should be established that is consistent with corporate personnel policy, organizational values, and organizational direction.

Instill and Improve

Many successful improvement activities are temporal. If the force that drives change or the leader who pushes for change is no longer present, the improvement methodology is often dropped and progress backslides into chaos again. Instilling the new way as *the way* is crucial for long-term sustainability. This is highly dependent on the culture and organizational system; however, the key is management commitment—commitment to lead the change, to implement the strategies, to model the desired behavior, and to stay the course.

All beginnings are difficult.

One of the key challenges is to just get started, as this German proverb points out. Rather than trying to design a perfect approach in a dynamic, adaptable system such as a large business organization, it will be more effective to start by improving the current system and then seriously and aggressively continuing to improve it.

In almost every case, once people gain adequate experience in the new lean strategic way, they will not want to go back to the old methods. It sometimes takes significant pressure to drive such a change; however, once a critical mass is achieved only minimal support is required to perpetuate it.

When embarking on a course of organizational improvement utilizing strategic alignment and lean methodologies, be certain that the part of the system on which you are exerting effort is worth improving! Many times organizations indiscriminately apply improvement approaches to all parts of the enterprise, like spreading peanut butter on a whole loaf of bread. For example, if a department, function, or activity is going to be eliminated, efforts on improvement should be limited unless there is significant economic impact prior to the elimination or unless the efforts will be used to train the people prior to redeployment. Communication, during and after the impact, should be managed to ensure management credibility.

Approach from Top, Bottom, or Middle

The optimum approach is a broad organizational involvement model that is initiated very quickly. Top management should set the specific direction, and they should be coaches for the organization. Therefore, they should be engaged in the change process first. It is crucial that once the change communication

begins that it be carried across the organization quickly. The quicker implementation can commence, the less time those opposed to the change (the organizational antiviruses) will have to mount an attack and resist the change.

Of course, change can be initiated at any level, at any size, and at any
speed. Figure 4.1 shows an impact model of organizational involvement and
the results. Selecting the right approach for the organization is highly dependent on the situational assessment factors that will be discussed in Chapter 11,
(and shown specifically in Figure 11.2).

Top Management Involved	Mid-Level Management Involved	Team Members Involved	Clear Reason to Change Recognized	Commitment to Stay the New Course	Results
√	√	√	√	√	• Sustainable progress
√					• Limited progress • Frustrated leaders
	√				• Minute progress • High supervisory frustration and resignations
		√			• Limited progress • Kernels of progress sprout and die
			√		• No progress • "We give up" attitude

Figure 4.1: Organizational Involvement Model

Selecting the Right Group

It was stated earlier in this chapter that broad involvement is usually beneficial. However, in most organizations it is impractical to involve everyone in all
activities. Therefore, one of the first challenges is to select the appropriate
team for the specific activity, and, for this, it is helpful to have a set of criteria
for team selection. For example, in large multifunctional organizations where
the activity will cut across multiple functions, it is usually beneficial to choose
representatives from each of the affected functions. A process concept is

shown in Figure 4.2 that graphically depicts the two major filters of functional representation and personality types.

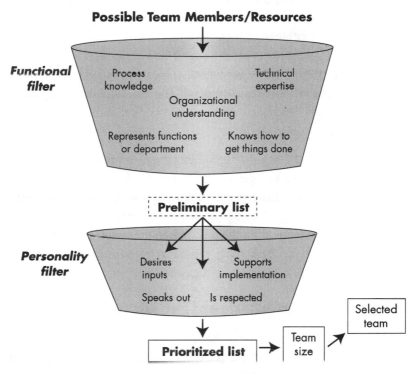

Figure 4.2: Team Member Selection Process

In selecting the functional representation, it is important to:

- Select representatives from each function or department, so each can have input into the improvement process.
- Consider including representatives from the supplier and customer organizations.
- Consider the functional capability of individuals. For example, do they:
  - Represent a function or department?
  - Possess organizational understanding?
  - Have process knowledge?
  - Have technical expertise?
  - Know how to get things done?

In considering the personalities, it is necessary to:

- Select representatives with participation-, team-, and results-oriented behaviors.
- Consider or include people who:
    - Want to be involved and desire input.
    - Speak out with good ideas.
    - Will actively support improvement implementation.
    - Have respect in the organization.
- Locate and include "informal leaders." These individuals are those who most people approach when peer-level direction is needed, and they make great team members.

The key point in selecting the right team members is to get a balance of functional representatives and personality types, while keeping the working team to a manageable size. Experience suggests that four to seven members is optimum. However, group sizes up to 20 have proven workable when the group behavior can be focused on the task. When the group of stakeholders is excessively large, a smaller task team can do the preliminary analysis and involve the larger group in review activities and/or other subgroup activities.

Value Add Versus Involvement Dichotomy

When involving a broad group of people, how much of the activity is non-value-producing or waste? The answer is sometimes stated as, "We cannot afford to involve a large group because we have too much real work to do." Involvement always has a cost and a set of benefits. The optimal level of involvement is unique for each organization and is highly dependent on the organizational culture. Answers to the following questions can help individual organizations decide what is best for them:

- How much of the activity is building the asset value of the organization for the future?
- How much of the activity is building support for implementation, which reduces future required effort?
- How much of the activity is just consuming people's time in a nonproductive way (wasting time and critical resources)?

The appropriate solution to this dichotomy is to maintain the proper balance of involvement—to add value while not having so much involvement that it creates waste, as shown in Figure 4.3.

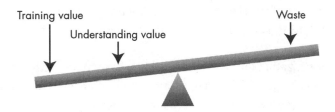

Figure 4.3: Waste versus Value Balance

Most organizations place some training value and some understanding value on organizational involvement:

- *Training value.* This is the building of organizational asset value through training of future leaders or preparing to address future needs.
- *Understanding value.* This is the building of understanding that allows for quicker implementation (and if not support for implementation at least reduced active blockage of implementation activity).

PERSPECTIVES

It is estimated that approximately 70 percent of dollars spent on training are wasted. Many corporations act like a marching band that is having difficulty with the piccolo section and decide that all band members will be fully trained in piccolo playing. This sounds silly, right? Well, how many of you have been trained in statistical process control (SPC), process reengineering, value stream mapping, design of experiments, quality, six sigma ... (*feel free to add in the ones from your organization*) ... or any one of hundreds of other corporatewide programs that you were never personally going to use or were not going to use in the near future? Lean organizations—those that understand waste and value—clearly target training to add value. A lean solution would be to provide intensive piccolo training just for the piccolo section (and any back-up people) and then, if necessary, provide a piccolo *awareness* communication for all of the other band members. This is exactly analogous to the business organizational situation. Lean, in this case, means getting just the right people involved at the right time.

The challenge is to select the right number of participants and the right participants, and to avoid going so far in involvement that it creates wasteful activity.

Many organizations have experienced involvement activities that created very little value. To gain high levels of value from organizational involvement, several aspects must be considered. First, the leadership and the culture must support employee involvement as an approach, and second, the organization must be operating in an arena where alignment of the organization can create additional value through faster or better implementation.

Many organizations estimate that over 70 percent of involvement activities are adding value when they are properly planned and implemented. The key aspects to carefully consider and to continuously improve include those shown in Figure 4.4.

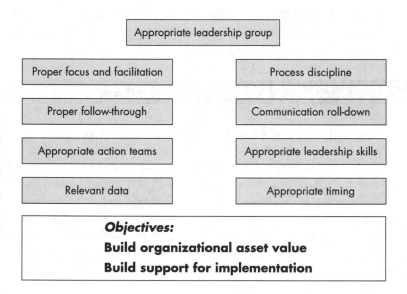

Figure 4.4: Aspects to Consider to Gain Value from Involvement

Involvement can create tremendous value when the required amount of alignment and support for implementation is high and when the involvement activities are focused and well managed.

Summary

The following quote highlights the importance of planning processes over the plans themselves:

"Plans are worthless,
but planning is everything"

Dwight D. Eisenhower—
U.S. Military General and President (1890–1969)

The process is absolutely critical to success. Whether planning or implementing improvements, it is always important to carefully consider the process and the constituents involved in building alignment—understanding, support, and commitment. Thoughtful implementation design increases the effectiveness of the activity and builds increased organizational understanding of the business situation, thus building future organizational leaders and improving the sustainability of the refined processes. Therefore, the magic is in *how* it is implemented.

5

Lean Management Systems Approach

Lean is so easy to discuss and so terribly difficult to do.
Lean means getting the waste out of:
  • *The way we do work (lean processes)*
  • *The work we do (lean content)*

The fundamental foundation of the Lean Management Systems approach is the focus on the reduction of waste. Lean principles have been very effective in many manufacturing operations; however, they are not limited to application only in the production environment. In fact, enlightened leaders have found that opportunities abound in nonproduction segments of the enterprise. Some examples of nonproduction areas that are ripe for improvement include:

- Development processes
- Time to market management
- Project selection processes
- Supplier management and relationships
- People motivation and creativity

Certainly, there are many other areas limited only by the imagination of those who wish to improve their organizations. It is easy to see that by reducing waste in developing new products and services, getting those products to market faster, selecting the optimum projects in which to invest, improving the supplier network, and reducing roadblocks to people's motivation and creativity yields tremendous dividends. When lean thinking is linked in an integrated manner throughout the organization, huge benefits result.

Lean Concepts

Lean is actually conceptually simple—it is a way of working that endlessly removes waste from any activity. Lean focuses on adding customer value and striving for perfection—never being satisfied that something is good enough or cannot be improved. The key focus areas (or objectives) of lean, as shown in Figure 5.1, are:

- Customer satisfaction.
- Value enhancement through waste elimination or reduction.
- Flow improvement—viewing everything as a process that supports creating value for the customer or the business.
- Speed—responsiveness enhancement and cycle time reduction.
- Flexibility—adaptability and the agility to be able to handle customer and market dynamics.

Figure 5.1: The Lean Focus Star

These five focus areas are intertwined and interrelated and are best implemented in an integrated fashion.

Lean Management Systems

Fully integrated Lean Management Systems (LMS) use the minimum people, time, and money to manage processes and accomplish tasks while communicating with, involving, and motivating the people throughout the organization. The Lean Management Systems process allows for the endless reduction of waste in every aspect and process in the organization. It causes an acknowledgment that waste exists, that waste is not acceptable, and that waste must be removed from the system. Lean Management Systems include:

- Lean plans—resulting in a clear strategic direction.

- Lean management processes—resulting in a documented management system and clear management processes.
- Lean business processes—resulting in lean flow, waste reduction in processes, and continuous improvement.
- Lean implementation—resulting in a structured and disciplined process to approve, communicate, and control the flow of people, money, material, projects, and activities—ensuring that strategies are implemented and goals are achieved.

The foundation for LMS is that organizations must be focused on creating value for their customers and their stakeholders, and that anything that is not adding value is waste. LMS focus organizations on this value-creation premise. LMS leverage the tools of lean systems, systems thinking, strategic planning, process reengineering, and team alignment to reduce waste in the five fundamental value-creating paths, listed below and shown in Figure 5.2:

- Leadership
- Marketing
- Development
- Production
- People

These five fundamental value-creating paths support the overall value stream of the organization—delivering a solution that meets the customers' needs. Managing the way in which these value-creating paths intersect and interact is critical to keeping the fundamental management system lean and functioning efficiently. How the organization actually does the work, communicates, and makes decisions among the value-creating processes is a significant indicator of management system "leanness." The objective of Lean Management Systems, when fully implemented and integrated, is to create a lean enterprise. A list of additional hints and attributes for a Lean Management System is shown in Appendix A as a detailed reference source.

In Lean Management Systems lean means utilizing people, material, and assets to achieve the optimum value of the total business system to generate maximum customer value and maximum business value in the minimum time and at the minimum cost.

The purpose of LMS is to create management operating systems that focus on the detailed processes shown in Figure 5.3,

The Major Value Stream

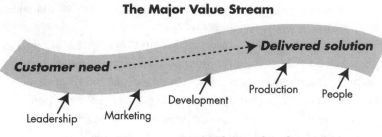

**Business success is driven by the
value added in all business processes**

Figure 5.2: The Key Value-Creating Paths Supporting the Major Value Stream

while reducing waste and increasing throughput. The fundamental management system of an organization provides and integrates these processes. It includes its rules, policies, procedures, and processes by which it carries out its business. Rarely do organizations consciously decide what their overall fundamental management system will be. Instead, it usually just evolves over time as the organization deals with situations, structure, personalities, and problems. Because it is so ephemeral, most people are unable to describe their own fundamental management system. Therefore, it is easy for waste to exist in this system without being recognized. If waste cannot be recognized, either due to a lack of definition or an inability by the organization to see waste, then the waste will not be challenged. Without challenging the need for continuing wasteful activity, organizations struggle to improve.

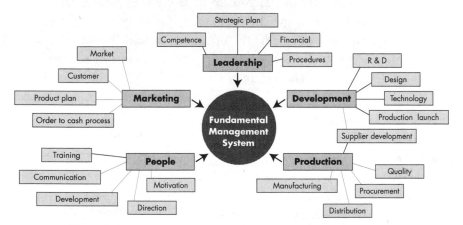

Figure 5.3: The Organization Creates Value Utilizing Many Processes
that Include Planning and Managing

While the focus for waste reduction is often on production, frequently the fundamental management system is at the root of the tremendous waste generated in organizations. Some simple thought-provoking questions, when honestly answered, reveal areas where waste is creeping (or galloping) through the organization:

- Is everyone in your team working toward the same goal set?
- Is everyone motivated to do his or her very best to help the organization win?
- Does everyone know the organization's goals with respect to his or her own work?
- Are organizational results more important than personal achievement?
- How well do the various groups in the organization work together?
- Are management systems set up to conserve resources?
- How much organizational time is spent waiting on decisions?
- Are management systems hassle-free and clear to everyone?

While most improvement processes focus on small, identifiable, and measurable improvements, often there is even greater opportunity to reduce waste in the leadership and controlling aspects of many organizations. This macrowaste (i.e., high-level waste that drives significant non-value-added activity across the organization) must be carefully evaluated, since the difference between a failed creative business development project and a wasteful management system activity may not be obvious upon initial evaluation.

The fundamental building blocks of Lean Management Systems (from Figure 3.3 in Chapter 3) are shown again in Figure 5.4, and the key lean business principles are shown in Figure 5.5. The building block model depicts the evolution of principles that build on previous concepts. However, specific concepts may be targeted, without the underlying building blocks in place, to drive organizational change or meet specific challenges. These two figures document the fundamental philosophy used throughout the Lean Management Systems concepts of this book.

There are many building blocks in the Lean Management System and each is important. However, some may provide more value in a specific situation or organization. As one begins to consider improvement, a thoughtful analysis of the situation combined with an understanding of the potential benefits of the lean building blocks and lean business principles should be undertaken.

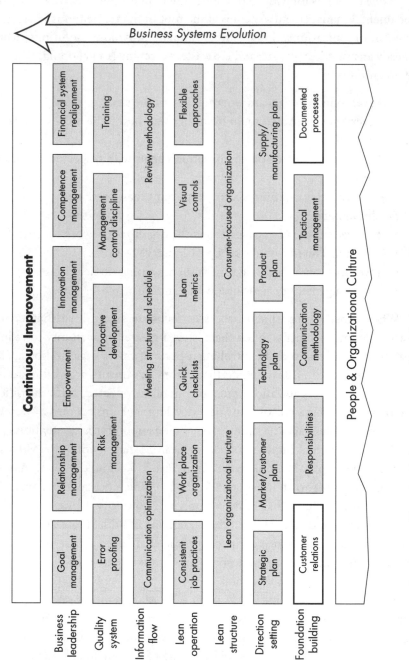

Figure 5.4: Business System Building Blocks in a Lean Management System

Lean Business Principles	Key Business Points
• Customer focus – Deliver what is needed when needed	• Powerful program/project management • Customer satisfaction focus
• Simultaneous development	• Proactive development
• Responsiveness to demand (flexibility)	• Applications, product development, and manufacturing development teams (support into stable production)
• Multifunctional workers	• Support for the worker, flexibility
• Visual management	• Optimized communication
• Consistent job practices	• Quality & efficiency through consistency
• Error proof—high risk areas	• Problem prevention and problem resolution
• Metrics	• Measures that drive desired behavior
• Staffing linearity	• Resource timing and competency
• Management cadence	• Lead-time management
• Cross-functional teams	• Teamwork, flexibility, & communication
• Direction & goals understood	• Aligned organization and policy deployment
• Maximum communication effectiveness	• Maximum communication—minimum communication volume

Figure 5.5: Key Lean Business Principles

Overview of the Lean Improvement Process

There is no "purple pill" that when swallowed will solve all the problems, remove all the waste, and create a lean enterprise. LMS is a concept that takes effort and must be tailored to individual organizations to match their business, vision, purpose, structure, philosophy, and culture. This tailoring to the specific situation is required to ensure that the improvement process itself is lean, and that the improvement is sustainable.

There are eight major requirements, shown in Figure 5.6, for an organization to follow to implement a lean cultural change. The first five requirements (gaining commitment, building involvement, training, focusing, and investing energy) are critical in getting started and overcoming the natural resistance to change. The last three requirements (building, striving, and rewarding) are required to maintain the lean philosophy and to embed it in the organization's culture.

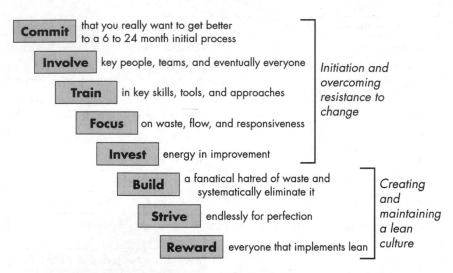

Figure 5.6: The Eight Requirements for Implementing a Lean Cultural Change

The general lean approach to improve an individual process is simple in concept, but complex in application, and typically includes the following six steps:

1. Understand the process or activity under analysis and its scope; create a flowchart of the steps in the activity (flow analysis).
2. Determine which steps add value, which do not add value but need to be done, and which add no value and can be eliminated (waste evaluation).
3. Determine the key metrics for the steps, including the time required.
4. Create a plan for improvement; consider the ideal state and create a desired state plan—eliminate, reduce, or combine activities.
5. Implement the planned actions.
6. Check progress and continually search for further improvements.

The first two steps of this general process define the two core techniques used in lean process improvement—flow analysis (flowcharting) and waste evaluation (value-analysis) and will be further discussed here. The remaining four steps are covered in more detail within the flow analysis and improvement process of Chapter 9 and Appendix D. In general these include: determining the key metrics for the process and steps (value-added time, wait time, quality, backlog, productivity, etc); creating a plan for improvement (documenting the step-by-step actions that will be done); implementing the planned actions (just doing the tasks); and checking progress (the key to continuous improvement is honest evaluation and continually searching for better ways). Many other lean techniques and tools are helpful in specific situations, such as workplace organization, visual controls, quick set-up, etc. These additional techniques provide detailed process guidance to further enhance the specific clarity of how to reduce waste and improve flow (see Chapter 11 for other techniques).

Flow analysis. Flow analysis is a well-understood technique that is also called mapping, process mapping, process flowcharting, value stream mapping, process blueprinting, or flow mapping, among others. The general flow analysis concept analyzes the flow of the current state (evaluating waste and time), creates an ideal state vision of perfection applying lean concepts, and then defines a desired state that will be the focus of implementation, as shown in Figure 5.7. Note that the desired state is most often a step back from perfection. It is much easier to create change in an organization by selecting a set of improvements that drive to the desired state, rather than trying to move directly from the current state to perfection. Each desired state implementation provides additional clarity on what the next desired state level should be. This allows the organization to make progress, grow, and learn. Inevitably, as progress is made the desired state definition should continue to move closer and closer to perfection, which is the continuous improvement philosophy.

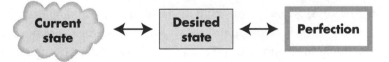

Figure 5.7: The Three States to Map

Waste evaluation. Of all the lean concepts, waste is usually the most difficult for organizations and individuals to grasp. Most of the activity that organizations work so hard to complete does not add value. The typical waste percentage ranges observed are from 50 percent to 95 percent for general management and administrative activities. Figure 5.8 shows the definitions for evaluating value-adding activities. These definitions should be taken to the extreme to

Value Add
Customer Value Add:
• Anything for which the customer is willing to pay
• Activities which increase the value of the material or service being produced

Business Value Add:
• Anything for which the stockholders want to pay
• Activities that build long term business assets

Waste
Waste to Eliminate:
• Anything for which the customer is not willing to pay
• Anything that does not support the needs of the business
• Anything that does not add value to the final product

Waste to Reduce:
• Activities that are currently necessary even though they do not add value to the customer or the business . . . until better methods are available

Figure 5.8: Value and Waste Definitions

help create a focus on waste reduction and improvement. (The terms waste analysis and value analysis are used synonymously throughout this book.)

Our concept of business value add was developed to address the fact that some desirable activities for the long-term business are not necessarily valued by existing customers. The following are examples of customer value add (i.e., activities that are valued by existing customers) and business value add. It is important to note that not all of the business value added activities would actually be adding value in every organization:

- *Customer value add.* These include machining, assembling, painting, creating designs, testing product to customer required specifications, packaging to customer specifications, etc. (Note: the customer is only willing to pay for placing the product into the box and closing it, but not for moving the part to the box, moving the box to the packaging area, or moving the packaged product to the customer's dock; also not for inventorying boxes or products, not for heating or cooling the packaging workplace [unless it is a specific product requirement], and not even for the packaging workers to have coffee breaks, etc.).
- *Business value add.* These include advertising to build market share, recruiting to have desired talent, training to improve skills, etc. (Note: the stockholders only want to pay for the portion of training that

actually adds value in the short term or adds asset value in the long term, but not for the travel costs to go to training, not for the time to arrange for the training, not for the time to complete the training request form or to fill out the expense report, not for the ineffective training time, and not even for the coffee breaks during training, etc.).

Most individual processes have some waste in them—some portion that is not adding value. Certainly most activities are not 100 percent value add, but some portion of them may add value that is desired by the customers or stockholders. Valuable activities must be targeted at doing the right things, and at doing those things well. As any activity is undertaken, careful consideration should be given to the specific details and content to maximize the value add.

The nine types of waste that should be eliminated or reduced are:

- **Physical waste:**
    1. *Overproduction.* Performance of tasks or functions not yet needed (when complete).
    2. *Correction.* Mistakes that require rectification or that circumvent the process.
    3. *Processing.* Performance of tasks or functions not necessary or that do not add value.
    4. *Motion.* Movement of people, materials, and information without a value-adding purpose.
    5. *Waiting.* Waiting on upstream activities, decisions, or approvals to be completed.
    6. *Conveyance.* Moving material or information from one place to another without adding value.
    7. *Inventory.* Storage and handling of material and information that cannot be used when processed.
- **Intellectual waste:**
    8. *Creativity.* Not using the creativity of everyone.
    9. *Motivation.* Not fully motivating everyone to perform his or her best.

The seven types of physical waste are based on the Toyota Production System definitions and the addition of the intellectual wastes is based on observations and discussions with clients about waste in their management systems.

It is important to note that waste is both physical and intellectual and that it can be found in any organization whether it is producing a product or providing a service. Waste can also be caused by specific behaviors and by the system. Both need to be addressed to truly eliminate the causes of waste. Every organization must live with waste until new methods can be designed, approved, and implemented. The challenge is to minimize the waste until it can be eliminated. (For reference, a survey process, a waste survey form, and a workplace organization survey form are located in Appendix A.)

Lean Management Systems Implementation Sequence

How does one eliminate the management waste and make the system lean? The implementation sequence to achieve Lean Management Systems (moving toward the lean enterprise) is listed below and diagrammed in Figure 5.9. Each step is more completely reviewed throughout the remainder of this book:

- Assess the situation and culture of the organization [Chapter 11].
- Orient the management team in Lean Management Systems principles [Chapter 5].
- Establish a lean strategic direction with a follow-up system [Chapters 6, 7, 8, 9, and 10].
- Establish key initiatives [Chapters 9 and 10] and:
  - Select the lean building blocks to improve (as shown in Figure 5.4) [Chapter 11].
  - Target detailed business processes to improve (reduce waste) [Chapter 11].
- Define and refine the management system [Chapter 5]:
  - Diagram, analyze, and improve the management system [Chapter 5].
- Implement initiatives and action plans [Chapters 10 and 12].
- Follow up and improve [Chapter 12].

In addition, the following process methods have proven helpful in many situations:

- Most organizations find it very productive to invest energy in developing and documenting their philosophies and values in conjunction with establishing their strategic direction. This is further described in Chapter 6.

- Establishing task teams to address individual initiatives and distinct process-improvement projects is a proven and effective methodology.
- Many find it helpful to establish a lean enterprise steering committee to oversee the implementation and set priority direction.

The techniques for lean assessment and the lean improvement methodologies are conceptually and practically intertwined. Most of the current state assessment techniques for lean also form the foundation for the next level of improvement. Therefore, it is difficult to separate the assessment discussion from the improvement discussion. Many organizations actually find it difficult to capture current state performance measurements, because once the assessment has begun people immediately see the waste and begin making improvements. Since positive improvement is the desired objective, this indicates organizational understanding and a propensity to take action. Properly guided, this can be a desirable outcome.

In implementing the Lean Management Systems approach it is highly recommended to simultaneously develop the strategic direction, the business system model, and the management control model. These techniques support common understanding and integrate well in terms of their assessment framework. These three items also provide clarity on targeting individual processes to improve through lean methodologies, because troublesome issues will be identified from these assessments. In addition, ensuring that the planning group has a firm grasp of Lean Management Systems concepts and that the plan undergoes rigorous lean design reviews will reduce management direction waste.

The Importance of Clear Strategic Direction

To truly gain the benefits of making the fundamental management system lean, organizational misalignment must be reduced to a minimum. Setting a strategic direction that is widely understood and supported is a critical step in reducing misalignment (see Chapter 7 for a more detailed discussion of the suggested process). The strategic plan and its proper implementation involves three steps:

1. Define the direction in which to go.
2. Get everyone knowing and supporting the direction.
3. Ensure that all actions support moving in the right direction.

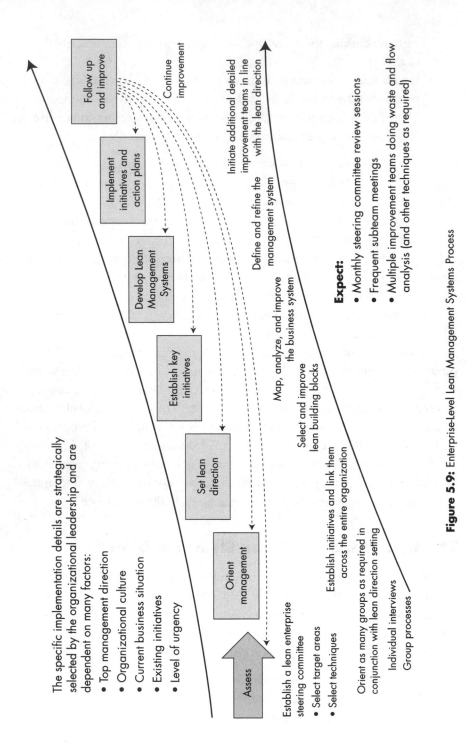

Figure 5.9: Enterprise-Level Lean Management Systems Process

This foundation provides clear guidance of future intent, what the boundaries are, what to consider improving, and what to ignore. Establishing a clear strategic direction is the key pathway to accomplishing lean content, or working on the right things.

Analyzing the Business and Management Systems

Three levels of analysis are suggested to cover the macro business system, the management system, and the detailed business processes of an organization. These analyses are the:

- Business system model (see Figure 5.10):
  - Macro models showing how the functional process blocks interrelate.
- Management control model (see Figure 5.11):
  - Model showing the process for overseeing and controlling the business system.
  - Many times depicted as the yearly schedule with controlling decision points.
- Business process analysis (see Figure 5.12):
  - Details of the business system showing key processes and the interrelationships (analyzed to as fine a detail as required).

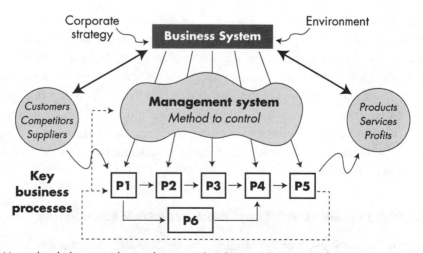

Many detailed steps within each process (see Business Process Analysis in Figure 5.12)

Figure 5.10: Business System Model

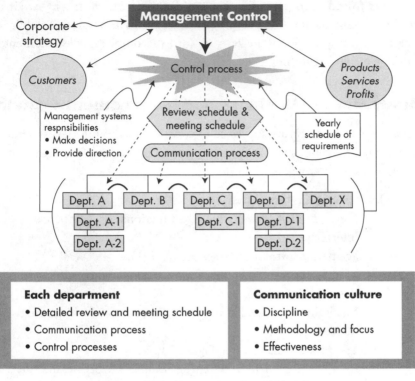

Figure 5.11: Management Control Model

The depiction of the business system model is a business system map, the depiction of the management control model is a management system diagram, and the depiction of the business process analysis is a process flow analysis. These models, maps, analyses, and diagrams are used to assess the current state and to visualize the ideal and the desired states as the improvement concepts are considered. These visual techniques aid understanding, clarify issues, assist in explaining to others, and provide a framework for analyzing potential improvements. The remainder of this chapter discusses each of these three techniques in detail.

Business System Map and Waste Evaluation

One of the first steps in understanding how the organization actually operates is to complete a business system map. First, the business system map is completed at a high-level perspective, and additional processes, linkages, and

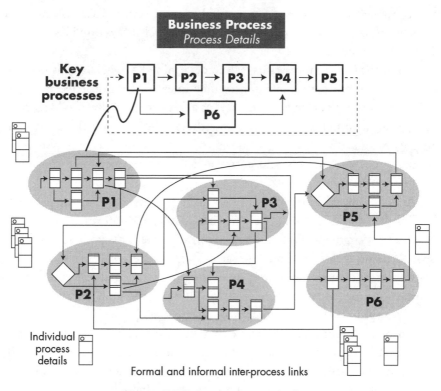

Figure 5.12: Business Process Analysis

interrelationships are added, as required, for clarity. The primary objective is to develop an understanding of how the organizational parts (functions, departments, or groups) operate as a system. A simplified view of the steps to developing the current state business map is to:

- Define the processes (or organizational parts) in the operation.
- Visually depict how these processes or parts interrelate.
- Document the attributes and key measures for the macro process.

The detailed worksheets shown in the flow analysis process (see Appendix D) and other traditional analysis techniques will be helpful as the analysis proceeds.

The optimum process for business system mapping starts at the top of the organization, and identifies the major business and management processes, both organization-wide and department- or function-specific. Consideration should be given to both the formal and the informal processes. Depending on the complexity of the organization and business, several layers of maps are often required. However, starting at the highest level always provides guidance for further analysis.

After the major processes have been determined, the next step is to create a business system map showing how they interrelate, as depicted in Figure 5.13. The business system is represented as a factory producing products, services, information, and profits. It shows these processes and the controlling management system to help instill the concept that the business system has inputs, processes, controls, and outputs—all of which need to be considered in the improvement activity.

It is not unusual for groups of knowledgeable and experienced people to find multiple ways in which the material, people, and information flow in a business system map—thus ending up with a spaghetti diagram. Charting the spaghetti and dialoging about the various approaches will enable the future improvement activities to address more completely the total system issues and interactions. Be sure to capture the key issues, trouble spots, and opportunities for improvement from these group discussions.

In order to eliminate the waste that exists in every business process; it must first be recognized, then the root cause must be identified, and finally the root cause itself must be addressed. A matrix evaluation is shown in Figure 5.14, which can be very helpful in organizing a group discussion on waste and clarifying the magnitude of improvement potential available—thus building recognition. This group discussion should take place after an introduction to the concepts of waste in the business and management system has been provided. This is an excellent activity to do in conjunction with the business system map, because it coalesces the impact of how well the business system really works—thus building additional understanding of potential root causes of waste.

The discussion on the business system evaluation matrix should link to the nine types of waste. In addition, injecting a few thought-provoking questions leads to a further depth of discussion and thinking about how well the business processes are actually working. A few examples of questions that help people internalize the true level of waste that exists are:

- How much of the activity is in crisis mode or late?
- How much of the work is done outside of the standard process?
- How much time is spent waiting on approvals, specifications, etc.?

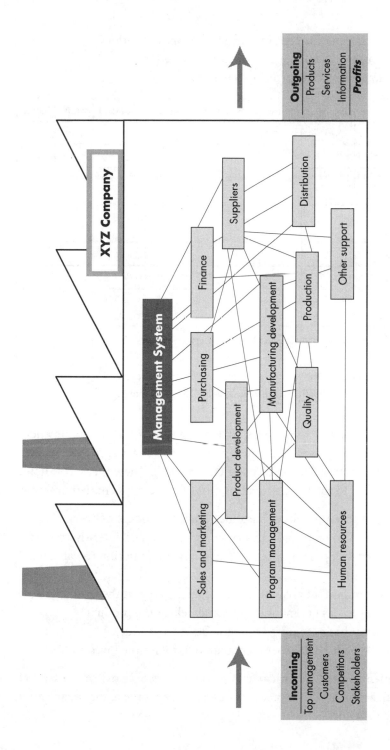

Figure 5.13: Simple Example of a Business System Map

- How much time is spent in intergroup communication?
- How much correction, or redoing, is required?
- How much special expediting is required?

	Process 1	Process 2	Process 3	Process 4	Process 5	Staff	Other
Employees**							
Budget **							
% Customer Value Add							
% Business Value Add							
% Waste							
Opportunity $							
Probability of Success							
Target $ Improvement							

** = Dedicated to this activity   Note: Process may be replaced by department

Figure 5.14: Business System Evaluation Matrix

Before beginning to improve the system design, it is highly recommended to document the key process attributes and at least the macro process measures across the organizational system for the current state. These measures should be directly related to the key deliverables of the business system. For example:

- Lead time from receipt of customer order to product delivery.
- Number of hours to process a large, repetitive, data-intensive report.
- Product development time from requirement definition to validated product.
- Number of hours to have a service representative at the trouble site.
- Total cost to design, manufacture, and deliver the product.
- Number of hours required to manufacture a product.
- Percent of value-added time compared to total time invested.

Documenting the key measures provides a scorecard of how much progress can be made with focused effort and helps motivate the organization to continue the effort.

IN THE REAL WORLD

During a management system analysis session, waste was being discussed and analyzed by a group of top managers. One of the managers said his department was 100 percent value adding because it had absolutely no waste. His group was hard working, spending on average nine and a half hours per person per day (being paid for eight) and that the work they were doing was absolutely indispensable to the organization. These perspectives always raise a red flag to an experienced lean consultant. Through further discussion it was discovered that this manager's group, although small, was established some years ago because customer prototype and preproduction parts were always late or wrong. His group's responsibility was to do whatever it took to get product to the customer when it was required—so they confirmed preproduction requirements and expedited parts delivery, sometimes through superhuman effort. This group valued this effort very highly and had pride in what they were doing for the company. It should be clear that this entire department was waste. It was a Band-Aid fix for a broken system. It was not possible for this manager to publicly confirm (admit) that his department and all the work that they did were not really adding value by the lean definition. He did make progress after some follow-up lean orientation and coaching dialogue, even admitting some waste, and as a result, began the improvement journey. It should be noted that it was very difficult for this particular manager to see the difference between the defined wastes in the department's activities and the need for these activities at all until the system itself was improved. After some additional sessions, the group began to focus on the new objective of making the standard system function properly, thus eliminating the need for this department.

Once the current state is defined, issues and opportunities that have been identified can be addressed and a detailed lean assessment can provide additional waste reduction improvements. The list of issues and opportunities identifies several subprocesses or process interactions that need to be improved through the detailed approach of business process analysis, or other supporting techniques. In creating the desired state for the business system, consideration of the ideal state is beneficial. Creation of the perfect business system concept can be challenging; however, a system without any waste is worth the

PERSPECTIVES

The business system evaluation matrix (Figure 5.14) can create quite a stimulus for conversation. It can be completed at various levels with various amounts of scientific research. We suggest completing the matrix the first time with a group without any preexposure. Provide the definitions of customer and business value add, and then begin a facilitated group process to fill in the chart. Allow all participants to help fill in the boxes at a rough preliminary level—so it can be done quickly. When people really begin to understand how much waste really is occurring in their respective departments, it then becomes possible to build their self-motivated desire to improve. Some groups will refuse to accept that they have been working very hard on something, perhaps for years, that is not 100 percent value-adding. Therefore, strong facilitation is highly recommended.

As a second step, consider having the people assess their work and the work of their departments for waste over a two-week time period. The waste survey sheet in Appendix A along with the waste definitions and types provide helpful guidance for reflection. Then conduct the second waste discussion, using the business system evaluation matrix, either by process, by function, or by department.

effort. In targeting where and how to attack waste reduction and improvement in the business system, it is important to select areas that will provide valuable gains, that will fulfill strategic needs, and that have a high success potential.

As the business system mapping process is followed, the future desired state map will be much more clear and orderly, and supporting processes can also be targeted for improvement as needed. Many times the business system map is only completed in a current state view, and is then used to target subprocess and process interaction issues for improvement. In this manner, it provides an excellent macroassessment process to prioritize detailed improvement targets.

Management System Diagramming

The management task is to approve, communicate, and control the flow of people, money, material, projects, and activities—that is, to provide direction and make decisions.

The management system is the process for achieving this direction in an organization. The majority of management systems have waste in the form of overcontrol, undercontrol, error prevention, redundancy, and conflict.

Lean Management Systems improvement begins by diagramming the what, when, and how of the management system. This is accomplished by documenting the responsibilities, major tasks schedule, schedule of reviews, meeting schedule, control processes, communication methodology, and organizational linkages, as shown in Figure 5.15. Management system diagramming is the process to capture and document the content of the management control model shown earlier, and it defines the requirements, cadence, and alignment methods for the organization. Figure 5.16 shows a simple example that may be helpful in clarifying the terminology. The discussion and understanding that evolve from the creation of this diagram is a significant part of its value. Therefore, it is important to ensure that the correct group participates in its creation and design improvement.

What? Requirements	**When?** Cadence	**How?** Alignment
Management responsibilities What are our management responsibilities? **Major tasks schedule** What are our major required tasks and their timing throughout the year?	**Schedule of reviews** What reviews need to be held to deliver on our responsibilities? **Standard meeting schedule** What meetings are required to accomplish our responsibilities?	**Control processes** How will we control that our good intentions are fulfilled? **Communication** How will we communicate to the organization? **Organizational linkages** What linkage and coordination with other parts of the organization need to be accomplished?

How do we run the business?

Figure 5.15: Management System Diagram Overview

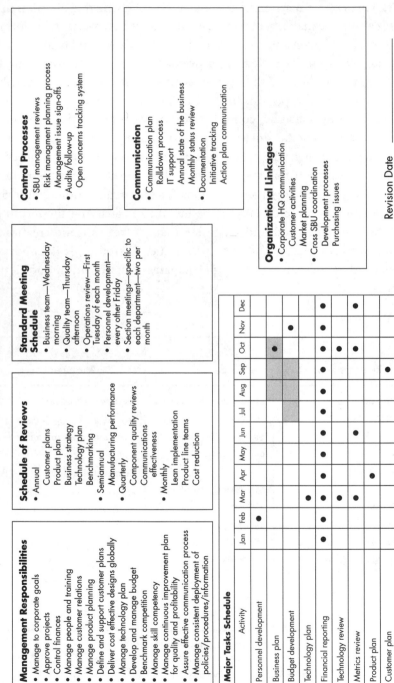

Figure 5.16: Management System Diagram Example

In creating the current state management system diagram, the following questions may provide additional clarity:

Management Responsibilities

- What are our management team responsibilities?
- Are there some required and some desired responsibilities?

Major Tasks Schedule

- What are our major required activities throughout the year?
- What are the key milestones (business plan, budget, etc.)?

Schedule of Reviews

- What reviews (approvals, critical evaluations, or information sharing discussions) need to be held to deliver our responsibilities?
- Which reviews require our participation to ensure we meet our obligations?
- How often are these reviews needed?

Standard Meeting Schedule

- What meetings are required?
- What events drive the requirement for meetings?
- Which meetings are we expected to attend?
- What meetings do we need to call?
- Which meetings are called as needed and which are regularly scheduled?
- How do we make these meetings meaningful, effective, and efficient?

The two areas that usually need additional clarification are control processes and communication processes. Therefore, the following lists may be helpful in building understanding:

Control Processes

How will we ensure that our good intentions are fulfilled?

- Identify methods used to verify that:
  - Processes are being used.
  - Metrics (goals) are being achieved.
  - Responsibilities are being met.
  - Projects are on time, budget, and target.
  - Communication is effective.

- Identify controlling methods:
  - Approval requirements and signatures
  - Management reviews
  - Paperwork requirements
  - Controlling procedures and policies
  - Audits
- Identify decision-making processes:
  - Decision drivers
  - Controlling authority
- Evaluate feedback system:
  - Timeliness
  - Effectiveness

Communication

How will we communicate to the organization?

- Determine what is communicated:
  - Data
  - Information
  - Decisions
  - Direction
- Determine when communication is required:
  - Regular and planned
  - Special events
- Identify the methods used to communicate:
  - Meetings (frequency, attendance, level of empowerment)
  - In-person/video/phone
  - Paper/e-mail/fax
  - Pager/voicemail
  - Internet and website usage
- Determine the level of communication effectiveness desired:
  - Stakeholder impact
  - Absorption and retention level
  - Sustainability of decisions
  - Organizational alignment around an established direction

Organizational Linkages

- What linkage and coordination with other parts of the organization need to be accomplished?
- What do we need to share, and with whom, across the organization?
- When is linkage communication required (prior—to gather inputs, or afterwards—to communicate results)?

The purpose of the management system diagramming process is to understand and document how the organization approves, communicates, and controls the flow of people, money, material, and activities. It answers the fundamental question, "How do we run the business?"

Once the current state is defined, issues and opportunities that have been identified can be addressed and a lean assessment can provide additional waste-reduction improvements. A few simple questions will quickly aid the assessment:

- How well does this management system work?
- How clear are the organization's responsibilities?
- How much of this activity is value adding and how much is waste?
- How can we eliminate or combine the activities?
- What activity can be delegated to a lower level?
- What key policies impact or interfere with what needs to be done?
- How can we improve these processes to make them better or faster?

With this diagram, it becomes much easier to visualize waste-reduction opportunities and the impact on the rest of the organization. Creation of the perfect (ideal state) management system diagram is problematic, unless the group is highly knowledgeable in lean thinking. Most organizations want to immediately design the new system once they begin to understand the waste and the opportunities. This will yield excellent results when:

- A lean design review is completed in a detailed, rigorous manner with knowledgeable people.
- A coherency check is completed to ensure that each responsibility has an approach or a process to address it, and that the control mechanisms are adequate, yet not wasteful.

The management system diagramming process can be applied at any level of an organization. Multilevel diagramming can be extremely powerful when the various levels are examined simultaneously, evaluating redundant, wasteful, and unclear activities. In this multilevel analysis, consideration should be given to the way the total management system interacts between the levels, and improvement opportunities should be explored.

PERSPECTIVES

The management system diagramming process can be applied at various levels of an organization from the CEO's office to the lowest department level. Examples of the types of issues that have been uncovered through this process include:

- Lack of clear understanding of responsibilities.
- Multiple meetings to address the same issues.
- Unnecessary meetings.
- Yearly calendars with most major activities crunched into a short time frame, rather than being evenly paced.
- Lack of advanced planning on known requirements.
- Haphazard communication processes.
- No connection between responsibility and action.
- Too many or too few control processes.
- Involvement in linkage and review meetings that were of limited value.
- Processes that violate company policy.
- Policies that were driving significant unrecognized waste.
- Control processes that cost more to run than the value of what they control.

Management system diagramming is a technique that highlights many opportunities for improvement and provides a great first step in recognizing management system waste.

This diagramming is exactly analogous to lean production planning, where we know the customer requirements, the takt time (the desired time between units of production output, synchronized to customer demand), the documentation requirements, etc. Through the use of lean techniques, the management system diagram can then be used to visualize a desired future state system with consideration to providing structure to the organization's management processes and cadence to the management schedule (takt time discipline).

Although it appears simple, management system diagramming can be complex and time-consuming. Many organizations require weeks to develop a clear first draft current state diagram. This process has proven to be extremely enlightening to many organizations, especially those that tend to get so consumed in doing the daily work that they lose sight of the simplicity of their responsibilities and how they are accomplishing them. In actual practice, lean improvement makes apparently complicated tasks much simpler—a major objective of Lean Management Systems.

Process Flow Analysis: Improving Detailed Business Processes

To create a lean system, the key business processes must first be identified. In determining the improvement priority of the key processes, their relative impact on the organization's performance and its strategic intent must be considered. In addition, consideration should be given to critical bottlenecks, largest waste areas (i.e., those that when eliminated would create the most dollar savings), opportunities to create organizational learning, ease of implementation, as well as long-term strategic importance. Many decision and selection tools exist to support numerical or subjective selection processes, from very simple to quite complex. It is highly advisable to use a method that has group support to build commitment to action.

When evaluating key business processes, it is usually better not to think only within departmental boundaries, because the key processes usually cross these lines. Evaluating processes within a department will allow for improvement of *intra*departmental processes, but will usually not allow for improvement of *inter*departmental processes. Interdepartmental interactions often create significant waste and result in suboptimization of processes within the functional departments. Since the causes of waste affect business processes throughout the organization, the impact of waste reduction can be leveraged significantly by approaching it systemically at a macro level, at the interdepartmental level, and at the intradepartmental level.

The improvement of detailed business processes requires rigorous analysis of the process steps, and is best accomplished through a flow and value analysis of the process at issue. Examples of a detailed flow analysis are explored in Chapter 9, which deals with providing a process structure, and a flow analysis process is outlined in Appendix D. Additional techniques to improve processes are covered in Chapter 11, which discusses technique selection and application.

The following list provides ideas and thought starters for processes that may exist in an organization and should be considered for improvement.

- *Leadership:*
  - Strategic direction-setting
  - Direction dissemination
  - Goal management
  - Competence management
  - Financial management
  - Organization structure
  - Communication (two-way)
  - Change management
  - Investment justification
  - Budgeting process
  - Policy and procedure management
  - Information systems
  - Implementation management and follow-up
  - Venture development and management
  - Business practice innovation
- *Marketing:*
  - Customer relationships
  - Customer support
  - Customer requirements capture
  - Market planning
  - Pricing
  - Order-to-cash process
  - Image and public relations
  - Advertising
  - Customer identification and selection
  - Project selection
  - Quotation management–planned and reactionary
  - Competitive assessment
- *Development:*
  - Development processes and structure

- Advanced development (research and development)—on both product and process
- Product development
- Design review
- Manufacturing development
- Quality assurance
- Supplier development
- Production launch
- Cost reduction
- Change review process
- Program management

- *Production:*
  - Manufacturing strategy
  - Supplier management
  - Supplier partnerships and alliances
  - Production scheduling
  - Manufacturing site selection
  - Union relations
  - Quality management
  - Production
  - Distribution and logistics

- *People:*
  - Philosophy and culture
  - Communication
  - Hiring
  - Development (training)
  - Compensation
  - Retention
  - Succession planning
  - Safety
  - Global diversity
  - Community involvement

The general process-flow improvement approach for targeted process improvement, from project definition to follow-up and ongoing improvement, is shown in Figure 5.17. The lean improvement methodology is very similar to the traditional process reengineering method, except that it requires a focus on waste and a focus on the perfect world with no waste to frame the development of the improved design. The lean improvement process is best conducted in small work teams (where practical, four to eight people), on specific areas, processes, or issues. The teams need to be empowered to develop substantive improvements. High expectations for these improvements need to be set for the teams. Larger groups are sometimes required, but efficiency and effectiveness are often compromised when a group gets too large.

Discipline in implementation and defined processes are critically important to successful process improvement. The reasons for this are obvious—if no system (i.e., processes and discipline) exists, it is very difficult to apply defined improvements that will last. If there are no processes, everybody can choose a different way to proceed. If there is no discipline to the process, everyone can choose which rules to follow. It should be clear that if employees do not follow process rules, then making new rules that will not be followed will be of little value. Establishing clearly defined processes and implementing them with discipline are core to improving the efficiency and effectiveness of processes and organizations.

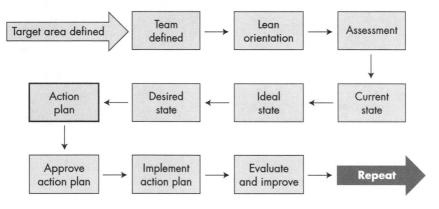

Figure 5.17: Process Flowchart for Targeted Process Improvement

One of the key improvement teams is the management staff of the organization. This team is responsible for the strategic direction and management system of the organization. Therefore, it targets the areas for improvement for the other teams, and ensures all implementation plans conform to requirements. This group also controls the speed of improvement by setting priorities, by providing supporting resources, and by providing inputs and feedback in improvement proposal reviews (stimulating creativity and motivation).

Summary

Lean Management Systems address the fundamental belief that intellectual resources are a key factor for the success of both today's and tomorrow's businesses. LMS use proven methods to reduce the waste of these valuable intellectual resources throughout the entire enterprise, and to gain results in all aspects of a business or organization, thereby moving toward the future objective of a truly lean enterprise.

Developing a fundamental management system that is lean, that allows for easy progress-tracking and redirecting, and that focuses the entire organization on adding value, can be accomplished through group sessions to improve the business management system (e.g., workshops that include training, management system design activity, and implementation planning). Four essentials for success in implementing a lean management system are:

1. Getting the management group aligned on the direction—with appropriate goals and processes.
2. Getting the management group to commit to the lean, continuous improvement philosophy.
3. Getting the management group to agree to track and show their progress.
4. Getting the management group to meet their commitments and accomplish action items.

Progress occurs only when action is taken. The point of LMS is to focus the time and energy of the organization on those things that add stakeholder value as well as to eliminate or reduce the time and energy spent on those things that do not add value. Once the Lean Management System is functioning as the essential way one does work, rather than as an added activity, then progress will begin to accelerate without continuous management intervention.

The general process recommended for creating a Lean Management System is:

1. Assess the situation and culture of the organization:
   a. Business system mapping and management system diagramming the current state provides additional guidance.
2. Orient the management team in Lean Management System principles.
3. Establish a lean strategic direction, with a follow-up system:
   a. Align the organization with the strategic intent.

4. Establish key initiatives:
    a. Select the lean building blocks to improve.
    b. Target detailed business processes to improve (reduce waste).
5. Define and refine the management system:
    a. Diagram, analyze, and improve the management system.
6. Implement initiatives and action plans.
7. Follow up and improve.

When designing management systems or business process improvements, it is highly suggested that potential system impacts and interactions be considered before implementing individual process changes. Caution should be exercised to implement improvement ideas that are focused on the impact to the whole system to prevent suboptimization and negative impacts that might help one area at the expense of the whole. Organizations should consider a group design review process before implementing improvements to reduce the risk of missteps. Careful consideration of the total system impact is critical in achieving better net results for the entire organization. With patience, perseverance, and commitment, there will be tremendous improvement in the leanness and the effectiveness of the organization.

NOTE

The next seven chapters are dedicated to further descriptions of the implementation details inside the Lean Management System. We have made the assumption that everyone will want to improve the leanness of their management system. The opposite of lean is fat, cumbersome, and chaotic. Certainly no one would wish to stay this way, nor risk their future expecting that the competition will be this way.

The Lean Management Systems approach does not define specific tools or techniques. It does suggest that the focus be on an integrated solution that minimizes the waste and maximizes the results. The LMS approach is an adaptive method that should be ongoing and continuously improving. The tools and techniques should be selected and applied based on the specific needs of the organization at the point in time they are required. Chapter 11 highlights numerous techniques that may be applied and reviews technique selection considerations.

6

Establishing Guiding Principles

Bomb diffusing instructions:
1. Remove access cover.
2. Break off green plastic clip to remove fuse relay switch cover.
3. Flip relay toggle switch next to the flashing red light.
4. . . . But first, cut the blue *wire!*

Many times, the establishment of guiding principles is treated like the blue wire step in these bomb-diffusing instructions. Typical instructions are, "Establish the organizational strategic direction and, oh, by the way, work on those philosophy and values things too! You know . . . those guiding principle things."

Philosophy and values may seem like soft and fuzzy topics, and working on stating the obvious may seem to be a waste of valuable time. However, experience demonstrates that early definition of values establishes boundaries for strategic direction discussions and enhances the clarity of what can be (and cannot be) considered when setting organizational direction. Those values that may appear to be obvious to everyone, often are not. When the CEO presents the philosophy and values of the organization at an all-employees meeting, and people start rolling their eyes, it is clear that the real philosophy and values of the organization have not been identified. A CEO who notes that behavior should not get upset with the people, but should recognize that there is work to be done.

Defining the values *first* yields great results:

- Time is saved up to 50 percent by setting direction.
- Many issues are identified early and can be addressed.
- Many conflicting directions can be avoided.

- Many of the "what we will consider" and "what we will not consider" decisions can be made philosophically.
- The true thinking that is guiding an organization is revealed.

Values Process

A very successful process for developing the philosophies and values of an organization is defined in the five-step process that follows. These topics should be addressed by the top management team, the organizational leaders, or the owners of a business.

1. Formulate the key statements that define the values of the organization. When formulating these statements, the following categories should be considered:

- Customers
- People
- Team members
- Business
- Competitors
- Quality
- Operations
- Service
- Profit
- Technology

IN THE REAL WORLD

While working with a client several years ago, we were engaged in a philosophy and values-setting session. We came to the subject of truth. One of the members of the management team said quite seriously, "We don't even need to address this subject because everyone knows that no one in this company would ever lie." There was a great deal of nervous laughter and incredulous glances among the balance of the people in the room. Finally, the CEO said, "Perhaps we ought to spend a little more time on philosophy and values. There seems to be a little gap between what we believe and what may actually be true."

- Product
- Purpose (Why does our organization exist?)

As groups discuss philosophies and values, many ideas arise that may not exactly fit the philosophy category. Typically ideas may also fit into rules of operation, strategies, tactics, or action plans. This is very acceptable, since these ideas can be sorted later in the process. Always document these ideas so that they can be reviewed at the appropriate time. This is depicted in Figure 6.1.

What do people always hear the management or experienced employees saying? Example: "Always take care of the customer first." This is a potential fundamental value.

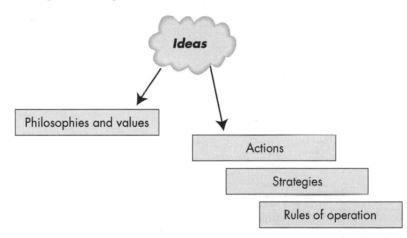

Figure 6.1: Philosophy Discussions Typically Generate Other Good Ideas

If additional philosophy categories are needed to stimulate thought, consider these:

- Change
- Subteams
- Leadership style
- Support for each other
- Openness
- Trust
- Integrity
- Teamwork
- Knowledge

- Discipline
- Conflict resolution/policy conflicts
- Decision-making and authority levels
- Ceremonies and events
- Communication
- Attitude

2. Determine how employees will accept these values and philosophies? Identify any potential gaps or issues that will require special effort to resolve.

3. Distill the preliminary list into the key items that are fundamental to how the organization behaves, or wants to behave, and sort out the ideas that are not philosophies. Three hints for this sorting process are:

- Keep the list short—include only items critical to describing how the organization will operate.
- Keep it credible—everyone must be able and willing to live by the values—always!
- Keep it understandable—the philosophies and values must accurately communicate intent to the organization.

4. Check for reality. It is not desirable to have meaningless statements that will not be followed. Will the management team be absolutely committed to adhering to the defined value set? If not, modify the statements to reflect what will be supported and implemented.

5. Run a test with random people in the organization or with small test groups (optional—but highly recommended). This can both determine organizational acceptance of the value set and belief that the management group will adhere to it, which can be very helpful in determining the best approach for communicating the results to the organization.

If the group is not able to have this type of discussion, an optional approach is to determine what the existing value set is by interviewing, either individually or in small groups, other people in the organization. This result may then be brought back to the leadership group, to determine whether it is as they wish it to be, and then adapted accordingly.

The best philosophy and values sets are a short list, not an encyclopedia. Some organizations like to create a long list, and then categorize the key items, and then end with a few fundamental values and a list of key philosophies. A conceptual example of this approach is shown in Figure 6.2.

Fundamental Values
- People: Treat all people fairly, consistently, and with respect.
- Business: Always operate with integrity and honesty and work to develop long-term relationships.
- Change: We embrace change as a way of life and welcome it as an opportunity.

Key Philosophies
- Customers: The customer is the only reason we exist. We will act as if our lives depend on our customers.
- Service: We will serve our customer better than we expect to be served.
- Products: We will strive to provide outstanding value that will surpass our customers' expectations and cause our competitors to react to us.
- Finance: We will maintain financial responsibility in all our dealings to assure that all our stakeholders are always treated fairly.
- Leadership: We will support positive leadership that is steady and consistent throughout the entire organization.
- Responsibility: We have the responsibility to protect and prolong the legacy of our organization and to protect our stakeholders to the best of our ability.

Figure 6.2: Conceptual Example of Values and Philosophies

Rules of Operation

Philosophies and values discussions usually generate a few solid rules that are not philosophy but are really policy. It can be very helpful to build this set of rules of operation and then add to it or modify it over time. These rules should establish clarity of expectation or determine the boundaries for the organization. Some typical examples are:

- We will meet every customer commitment (if we cannot meet the commitment, we will let the customer know in advance with a recovery plan).
- All meetings will have a preplanned agenda and documented action items.
- All development prototypes will be error-proofed by the engineering quality department before release to customer shipment.
- All price quotations will be signed off by the pricing manager before going to customers.

- Only sales and marketing personnel will provide pricing information to customers.

Rules of operation should be absolutes that have 100 percent conformance expectation. In a lean management system it is desirable to have as few rules as necessary to define the requirements, while allowing flexibility to be responsive in completing tasks by following the defined lean processes.

IN THE REAL WORLD

A client firm that was in deep trouble in its market and had organizational conflict decided to undertake a new lean strategic direction. In the very first meeting in an operations tour, a large "Our Philosophies" sign was observed. The sign read:

> ### Our Philosophies:
> - We believe in people
> - We love our customers
> - Quality is our mission
> - We always deliver

The company had just furloughed 20 percent of its employees, had missed many customer shipments, had knowingly shipped parts with quality problems, and was holding a customer hostage over a billing dispute. After a few pertinent questions to the CEO, it became clear to him that this sign was not representative of their current behavior, so he immediately called for a ladder and personally removed the sign. This was an epiphany for him. He then decided to begin a new age of management—by saying what they meant and doing what they said. He committed the next eighteen months to changing the behavior of his organization. When he was satisfied that the organization was truly following the philosophies that were desired, he scheduled a sign-hanging ceremony and replaced the original sign. Many of you may have experienced signs like this as well. Hopefully they are also no longer hanging if they are not representing true behaviors.

Management Credibility

It is absolutely crucial in creating management credibility that the published values are followed religiously. When organizations publish platitudes that they never intend to fulfill, they absolutely destroy management credibility and sow the seeds of cynicism in the organization. When management publishes statements that they do not intend to follow, they invite employees

IN THE REAL WORLD

One of the most meaningful revelations of our industrial experience was a lesson on the importance of clear and concise management direction and credibility of management. This experience resulted from working on a significant project with Toyota. The short version of the story is as follows: The Toyota coach, while standing in a hallway intersection, asked the type of question that Toyota *senseis* ask so well and so innocently, "What is the management direction to the team members (employees) here?" Pointing at the escalator coming *down* toward us, the sign clearly read, "Please Hold Handrail." The Toyota coach grabbed the down-moving handrails to follow the management direction. Of course, he immediately was dragged to the floor (escalator coming down). Looking up he asked, "Is this what management wants?" The answer was, "Of course not."

In this case, the escalator's direction had been changed and the sign had not been moved. It was clear that he knew that employees were smart enough to realize that they should use their judgment and ignore the direction in the sign.

After some discussion, he asked a follow-up question, "So if management does not expect the team members to follow this direction, but to use their own judgment—how do the team members tell which management directions to follow and which to ignore?"

He then postulated that the management direction might lack credibility with the team members.

We have since experienced the many aspects of lack of management clarity and credibility in many organizations. Reaffirmation of the real requirements, and a refining review of operational policies with communication to the organization, can be extremely helpful in the early stages of rebuilding management credibility.

Establishing values and philosophies—the guiding principles of the organization—is crucial to creating management credibility.

to ask themselves, "What other management direction is everyone allowed to ignore?"

In order to have values that help the organization, these values must be real. They must be commitments. They must be met every time. Being true to the values statements is one of the great tests for management credibility and one of the most direct ways to build respect for management.

Summary

The time invested in discussing and sorting out the key philosophies and values of an organization is tremendously valuable in defining organizational strategic direction. When the leadership group confirms and commits to implement a set of values and then really stands behind them, management credibility is greatly enhanced. This will establish a foundation for all further improvement and for implementing the organization's strategic intent. A well thought out, lean set of rules of operation can provide tremendous clarity on the absolutes of management.

Healthy organizations have the openness to help remind each other to stay consistent with the values set as they progress through difficult daily activity. This open self-policing, along with acceptance from the receiver of the input, creates deeper commitment to the values and sets a tremendous positive example for the organization.

7

Implementing Strategic Direction

The first step is to decide what one wants to accomplish. If you do not care where you are going, any path will take you there...

"Would you tell me, please, which way I ought to go from here?"
"That depends a good deal on where you want to get to," said the Cat.
"I don't much care where—" said Alice.
"Then it doesn't matter which way you go," said the Cat.
"—so long as I get SOMEWHERE," Alice added as an explanation.
"Oh, you're sure to do that," said the Cat, "if you only walk long enough."

From *Alice's Adventures in Wonderland* by Lewis Carroll.
(Lewis Carroll was the pen name of Charles Lutwidge Dodgson, 1832–1898)

Use of strategic planning has been like a swinging pendulum over the past 30 years. It has been in favor one day and out of favor the next. New names, new twists, and new marketing approaches to sell the benefits of strategic planning have created a virtual grab bag of alternative approaches. In many organizations, strategic planning morphed into a bureaucratic activity created for the benefit of the strategic planners who made vain attempts to predict the future. While these approaches deserve much of the derision that they have received, the benefits of creating a clear strategic direction and aligning the entire organization around it are undeniable.

Most organizations do not have the luxury of *"walking long enough to get somewhere;"* therefore, most insightful leaders truly appreciate the value of having a clearly conceived and thoroughly documented strategic plan.

When creating a lean and focused organization, one of the first questions is always, "What is this organization trying to accomplish?"

The answer requires you to address the right priority issues in any organizational improvement. The answer can be clearly determined through strategic planning and strategic organizational alignment processes.

The concept of aligning an organization through strategic planning is quite simple. The successful implementation process is complex but absolutely worth the investment. Setting an overall strategic direction that is widely understood and supported is a critical step in reducing misalignment. As we noted in Chapter 5:

1. Define the direction in which to go.
2. Get everyone knowing and supporting the direction.
3. Ensure that all actions support moving in the right direction.

The fundamental purpose is to focus the time and energy of the organization on those things that add stakeholder value and, of course, to eliminate or reduce the time and energy spent on those things that do not add value. Strategic direction-setting is a tremendous tool for making the content of the organization's activities more lean. Many lean approaches focus on improving the existing processes; however, it is also important not to waste time imposing lean practices on activities and processes that do not support the strategic direction of the organization. The ten points of successful strategic management and alignment that build the capability to implement lean management systems are:

1. Create a vision.
2. Develop management commitment and align everyone's actions to reach the vision.
3. Establish a crossfunctional approach to run the business.
4. Establish clear strategic plans with measurable goals and specific initiatives and actions.
5. Ensure that responsibilities are assigned and understood.
6. Provide leadership, empowerment, and coaching.
7. Use an open communication process to create awareness and understanding of the business.
8. Establish a management process to ensure progress on the plan.
9. Create a high responsibility, participative, "no fear" environment that encourages teamwork.
10. Recognize and reward results and valiant attempts (i.e., reward people for doing the right things).

What Is a Strategic Plan?

Plans come in various shapes and sizes, but understanding what makes a plan strategic is important. Any complete plan always includes basic elements such as a vision of some desired results, a chosen set of strategies and tactics, and an implementation approach. Everyone has developed this type of plan. Maybe such a plan was used in deciding something as important as where to go to college or something as mundane as where to go to lunch. In either case, it is a simple plan, but it is not a strategic plan.

This type of plan is very narrow in scope, internal in focus, and single-issue in orientation. Strategic plans are broad in scope, multidimensional in issue orientation, and both externally and internally focused. The external focus is usually on customers, competitors, suppliers, markets, new opportunities, and threats, while the internal focus is on implementation, capability, and competence.

Strategic plans successfully integrate the market and technical direction of the organization, while guiding the selection of products and services that will be offered. They must also deal with how the products or services will be supplied, what resources will be required, and what the expected financial results will be (Figure 7.1). There are many business practices that can be affected by strategic plans and their supporting actions. See Chapter 5 (pages 70 and 71) for a listing of critical business processes to evaluate while developing an integrated strategic plan. In first-class strategic alignment processes, the implementation methodologies are integrated with the organizational cultural system to increase both success rates and sustainability.

A strategic plan starts by considering the environment and its impact. It considers such environmental factors as what current and potential customers want and do not want, what competitors are doing or are likely to do, what impact will government regulations and laws have, what scientific developments may change the game, and many more. Only after considering the relevant environmental factors and the organization's position relative to them, through a rigorous self-assessment, can one begin to answer the simple question, "Where are we?"

Typical organizations have multiple functional groups or departments. The environment may affect each function differently, and true success will require that these different groups work together. Therefore, it is important for strategic planning to be a multifunctional activity involving the leaders of

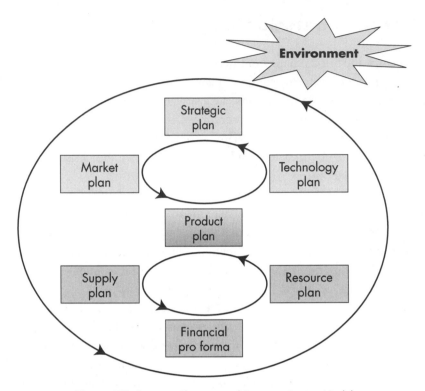

Figure 7.1: Business Planning and Direction-Setting Model

the various parts of the organization. This not only provides multiple points of view, but it will later provide a means to cascade the plan down and spread it throughout the organization. Each group's activities can then be guided by the integrated plan.

A strategic plan considers the interests of the stakeholders. These include entities both inside and outside of the organization such as employees, owners, customers, suppliers, and the community. Dealing with misalignment of stakeholder interests is a major challenge for most organizations, but the consequences of not addressing it can be severe. Boards of directors may force CEOs to step down, unions may disrupt the groups for which they work, and customers may discard longtime suppliers.

Unlike the simple, single-issue plan, a strategic plan must align all the dimensions of the organization in working synchronously toward reaching the agreed upon goals. Therefore, a strategic plan requires a thorough description of where the organization wants to be in the future. Without understanding the organization's principles, beliefs, and values (as discussed in Chapter 6), and without a clear concept of what it wants to be in the future, it will be impossible to synchronously work toward the vision in all parts of the organization. Without a widely held, common understanding, well-meaning people in different parts of the organization will embark on paths that are counterproductive, which will reduce the ability of the whole organization to meet its goals.

In a strategic plan, the strategies and tactics are the approaches used to reach the goals. They are based on the opportunities and limits of the environment and the capabilities and strengths within the organization. Building winning strategies depends on truly understanding the key success factors that are present and the ability of the organization to deal with them. There are many possible strategies that can lead to an organization meeting its goals. Choosing a winning set of strategies depends on the unique positioning of each organization relative to its environment, as well as the capabilities, strengths, and weaknesses that the organization possesses. In other words, what may be a good strategy for one organization may not be good for another one.

A strategic plan has a specific implementation associated with it. Tactics, action plans, programs, or initiatives are associated with each of the strategies and goals, timing is set, resources are allocated, and responsibilities are assigned. By doing this, the various parts of the plan and the required actions of the organization can be integrated into the overall scheme. Follow-up and success-tracking become possible, and how well the plan is working becomes clear. This allows for replanning as necessary when situations change or when it is realized that the current plan is not working as originally intended. Accordingly, a strategic plan should be treated as a dynamic plan that is updated and adjusted when appropriate.

When the environment is changing rapidly such course corrections must be made to accommodate changes in a timely manner. With a solid strategic plan as a basis, reactive course changes will not be required, as the plan creates a foundation of stability from which to make corrective changes.

Strategic Questions

A strategic plan answers four fundamental questions:

- Where are we?
- Where do we want to go?

- How are we going to get there?
- Are we making any progress?

These are shown in Figure 7.2 with their related implications in the language of strategic planners.

Laymen's Language	Planner's Language
1. Where are we?	• Environmental assessment • Market analysis • Mission
2. Where do we want to go?	• Vision • Key success factors • Objectives and goals
3. How are we going to get there?	• Strategies • Tactics, action plans, programs, and initiatives
4. Are we making any progress?	• Appraisal of: – Goals met – Actions complete – Strategies working – Intended results accomplished

Figure 7.2: Language of Planners

The general approach of strategic planning processes is simple in concept but complex in application and generally includes the steps shown in Figure 7.3. To answer the first question—"Where are we?"—a concept of the organization's place in the environment is needed. The organization must understand its present and potential customers, their needs, and their key buying factors. An understanding of the organization's strengths and weaknesses relative to its competitors and suppliers is also a must. The organization must be able to discriminate important market factors, and their attendant opportunities and threats, from the unimportant. The organization should examine what it offers, what it needs, and its key success factors. There must be a match among these items and the organization's fundamental values. This understanding of "Where are we?" can be organized into a holistic group of inputs called the concept model.

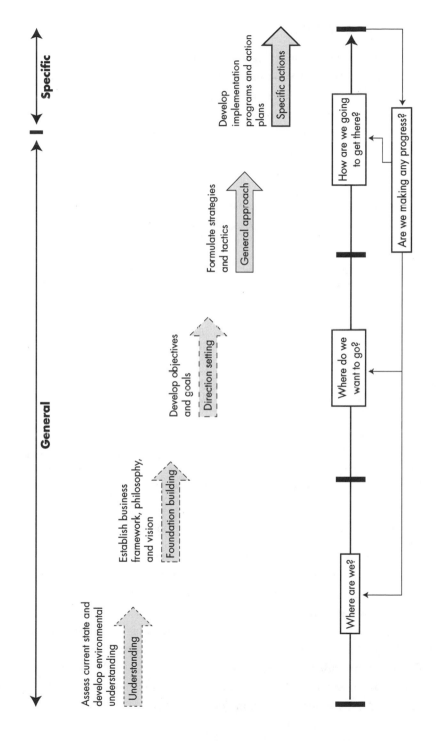

Figure 7.3: Stages of Planning

The Concept Model

The concept model, shown in Figure 7.4, is best completed in a group discussion of knowledgeable people, since it is designed to capture the group's concept of how the business operates (or needs to operate). It is to be completed as a processed list with a high level of group agreement. The concept model can be considered an environmental assessment. The lower section of the concept model is the traditional marketing tool known as the SWOT (strengths, weaknesses, opportunities, and threats) analysis.

Concept Model					

Customers	Customer needs	Key buying factors	Key success factors	Company needs	Products

Competitors	Strengths	Weaknesses	Opportunities	Threats

Figure 7.4: Concept Model Format

A few additional hints for using the concept model process are:

- Address the top row from the outside edges inward; that is, first, customers and stakeholders, second, your products, third, customer needs, fourth, company needs, fifth, key buying factors, and sixth, key success factors.
- Address the bottom row from left to right beginning with competitors.
- It is important to look for linkages *across* the model categories, *not* down the individual category lists.
- The "Customers" category can include real (external) customers, stakeholders, and internal customers as required.

- The "Products" category can include the products that are supplied and the related services that support the products but for which there is not a direct charge (e.g. application engineering), services for which there are direct charges, and other items of support on which customers place value.
- Key buying factors give insights into approaches to customers. The "Key buying factors" category is meant to define the key factors on which customers actually make their buying decision. For example, given equal performance, price, quality, and delivery—what criteria does the customer use to decide?
- The "Key success factors" category is the distilled, short list of significant aspects that when implemented will drive organizational success.
- In defining objectives, carefully consider customer needs and company needs.
- In defining strategy, be sure to address key success factors.
- It is often helpful to consider strengths and weaknesses relative to key competitors.
- The concept model is intended to be considered in its totality to aid in developing understanding; therefore, it should be shown on one page for visual impact.

The concept model allows planners to develop insights into their organization with respect to both internal and external factors. Additional forms, formats, and definitions are in Appendix B to support strategic planning processes.

The concept model is based on the belief that concept precedes experience, as espoused by Russell Ackoff (author of *Creating the Corporate Future* and other books on systems thinking). Often groups make the mistake of attempting to lay out their specific objectives and goals prior to understanding the purpose of today's organization (mission) and prior to having a concept of what the organization intends to be in the future (vision). As Ackoff has pointed out, one cannot truly experience something until they have a concept for it. It is extremely difficult to ask an organization to experience their strategic direction before they have a concept of what they want to be, yet this is exactly what many try to do. When developed correctly, the concept model allows the planning group to delve into the interrelationships that the organization creates in its interactions with its stakeholders. Often times an analysis of the environment in which the organization functions does not yield a good concept of how the organization interacts with its environment.

However, creating a thorough concept model has repeatedly proven to be effective in helping organizations gain insight into how they fit into their environment. Thus, they develop a concept for their organization.

Strategic Plan Design

The entire strategic plan design is shown in Figure 7.5. This figure shows how the elements flow in a stairstep fashion from the concept model.

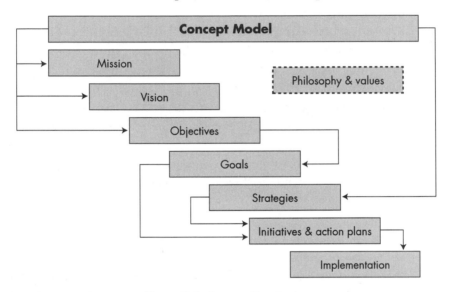

Figure 7.5: Strategic Plan Design

Mission. From this concept model foundation, the organization can formulate its mission or what it stands for today. The mission should answer the questions who, what, and how:

- *Who:* Who do we serve? Who are our customers? Who are our stakeholders?
- *What:* What do we offer? What are our products? What are our services? What are the soft services that help to differentiate us from the competition?
- *How:* How do we do what we do? How do we approach winning the game?

While a mission statement is often reduced from a meaningful description of intent to a nearly meaningless, simplified slogan, a true evaluation of the mission of the organization is invaluable in understanding how an organization truly operates and for what it stands. Most have seen such slogan-like mission statements as: We will provide the highest value to our longstanding customers through the delivery of the highest quality products and services.

This statement provides little value in truly evaluating where the organization is today, but thoroughly answering these three questions will provide significant insights for today's organization. For example, by thoroughly examining the customers served (and not served) the field of competition (from the organization's point of view) has now been defined. By noting the products and services that are offered, the organization has now defined the limits of what it provides (and does not provide). By briefly describing how the organization intends to win, it will be able to define the basis for its competitive advantage. It will also be able to define what winning means. It often

IN THE REAL WORLD

Many years ago we worked with a client organization that had been very successful in the past, but that was moving into a period of stagnation and unacceptable financial results. This client was extremely internally focused, had little regard for its customers, and was rather arrogant. While assisting them in a mission evaluation, we had great difficulty in getting them to recognize their true current position. Finally we created a mock mission in an attempt to shock them into recognition. Our mock mission read:

We make stuff and allow our customers to take it off our hands if they will give us enough money and come take it off our docks.

At first, they laughed uproariously, but then slowly the laughter faded, and they began to realize the intended impact of the statement. One of the members of the management staff said, "That's funny only because that *is* the way we would like to behave. If that's the way our customers see us, we have big problems."

Certainly no one would write a mission statement like this one. We were able to begin making progress on improving the situation by examining the elements that make up a mission and shocking the management group with a mock mission.

does not mean the same thing to everyone in the organization. While no one sees much value in creating mission statements like the slogan-like one previously stated, it is easy to see the value in a thorough examination of the elements. When this is done with enough rigor, the organization gains focus on where it has placed its boundaries, and it begins to identify some of the implications of those boundaries. After all, most organizational boundaries are set by organizations themselves. Therefore, they can move the boundaries if they choose to do so, but first they have to recognize where they are.

It is surprising to note how few organizations spend time really contemplating which customers they serve, and why they serve this set of customers. The same can be said about the products and services that organizations offer. By answering why we serve customer A, but not customer B, and why we offer Product 1, but not Product 2, we obtain insight into what the organization is today. For those who are attuned, it also begins to provide insights into what the organization could be if it chose to be different than it is today. When the mission of the organization is analyzed or developed in this way, it is truly a value-added activity.

Vision. Where do we want to go? To answer this question the organization must start examining possibilities, which are usually practically unlimited. The organization must create its vision of what it wants to be in the future. It may be very similar to the current mission or it could be quite different, but this is how the organization begins to define its business and its future direction. Defining a motivating, ennobling vision that really challenges the organization to make progress can be extremely valuable in supporting organizational alignment and building support for implementation.

The vision addresses the questions of who, what, how, where, and when. While the first three questions are the same as in the mission, they are now in the future tense:

- Who will the organization's customers and stakeholders be in the future?
- What products and services will be offered in the future?
- How will the organization win the game in the future?
- Where will the organization physically be located in the future? Where will the organization's customers be in the future?
- When will the organization make the transition from what it is today into what it intends to be in the future?

Like the mission statement, it is not the vision *statement* itself that is critical. It is the thorough examination of what the organization intends to be that is critical. This is where the organization begins to decide where the new boundaries will be. The organization should thoroughly understand the implications of what is different when comparing the mission of today and the vision of the future. It is the understanding of these implications that provides insight into required actions to move the organization along the appropriate path.

Objectives. By examining the gap between its current mission and its future vision, the organization can assemble objectives that it will strive to meet. These objectives more specifically describe the vision and serve as the basis for what the organization wants to be and where it wants to go in the future. In addition, it is helpful to consider the "Customer Needs" and "Company Needs" inputs from the concept model. Objectives are usually few and very long term in nature.

Goals. Associated with each objective is a set of goals that further define the objectives. These are more specific in nature, and usually shorter term in focus. Goals are not a statement of well being. They must be measurable and specifically define the expected results (e.g. reduce cost by 5 percent), and they must define the deadline for the expected results (e.g. within 12 months). An organization needs to know whether it has met its goals, and it needs to assess whether the goals were appropriate. Goals serve as mileposts against which progress will be measured, and indicate whether the strived-for objectives are being approached. If a group of people were dropped in a desert, their objective might be long-term survival. Their goals might be to find water within 24 hours, to find shelter from the sun within four hours, and to get out of the desert before they starve or fry! Goals are discussed in more detail in Chapter 8.

Strategies. In Figure 7.6, an example of vision, objectives, and goals are shown, along with a set of strategies for a business-to-business supplier organization. This is not intended to be the complete set of objectives, goals, and strategies. However, it is intended to show that the goals line up with their associated objectives, but the strategies do not necessarily line up one for one. Each of the four strategies shown will support accomplishing the objective of profitable growth, but they will also support accomplishing other objectives, such as offering new technology to the marketplace, having cost-competitive

Vision: Be the global leader of providing widgets to market leading customers focusing on Europe, North America, and Japan by always providing the best technology first.

Objectives

O-1 Have ongoing profitable growth.

Goals

G1.1 Achieve a global market share of 30 percent within three years.

G1.2 Achieve before tax profit of 15 percent on all new sales.

G1.3 Capture new business at one new customer in each geographic market for each of the next three years.

Strategies

S-1 Invest in new technology and be first to market in Technology A, B, and C.

S-2 Focus growth efforts in Europe and Japan.

S-3 Invest in low-cost manufacturing with a global footprint.

S-4 Empower all employees to improve processes.

Figure 7.6: Strategic Plan Vision, Objectives, Goals, and Strategies Example

manufacturing, and having satisfied employees. The strategies, taken as a set, should support accomplishing the set of objectives and goals.

Dealing with the question of how to proceed toward the vision involves the process of strategy formulation. The key success factors developed in the concept model stage provide guidance in developing winning strategies and determining what should be done. Understanding the environment provides insight into what might be done. Actions of competitors determine what must be done. Resources of the organization limit what can be done. Sorting through this to determine the appropriate set of strategies that will be used is critical to beginning the implementation process. Many want to jump to this step before they have really determined their true objectives and goals. However, this is like someone in Chicago jumping in a car and heading south before they have determined that their goal is to be in Alaska the next morning! Much waste is incurred this way, as the scarce resources of the organization are used on actions that are not aligned with the direction in which the organization needs to go.

Creating the strategies that provide for successful implementation of the strategic plan can be extremely difficult. Creating objectives, goals, and action plans can be done in a logical, deterministic approach. By following a logical process, the appropriate objectives and goals can be determined, and action plans can be created. On the other hand, strategy development is a creative process and cannot automatically be deduced in a deterministic methodology. Logical, stepwise processes can be and should be followed (see Figure 7.7), but they will not necessarily lead to successful strategies.

The search for the perfect strategy is endless.

Successful organizations constantly evolve their strategy and tactics to be successful global competitors. Their success in providing products and services quickly and profitably in a rapidly changing market is driven by managing according to an integrated, dynamic understanding of the elements of the strategy creation model shown in Figure 7.8. It is clear that the search for the perfect strategy will be endless as the environment changes and the organization evolves.

When creating strategies, many questions should be considered:

- What degrees of freedom does the organization have?
- How should the organization use its assets to gain advantage over its competitors?

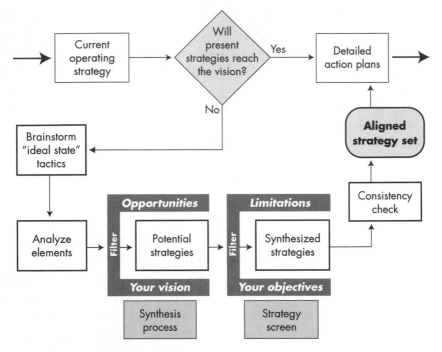

Figure 7.7: Creative Strategy Development Process

- What seem to be the strategies used by the organization's competitors?
- How will the organization's strategies work relative to the competitors?
- What should the organization's strategy be relative to product innovation—leader, fast follower, slow follower?
- What will the fundamental manufacturing strategy be—high capital with low labor content at a high compensation rate, or low capital with high labor content at a low compensation rate?
- Where will facilities be located—distributed close to customers and focusing on being super responsive, or concentrated in one or two locations and focusing on economies of scale?

These are just a few of the questions that should be considered as the organization starts to create its strategies. The chosen strategy set must fit the capability and the competence of the organization and must be aimed at achieving what the organization has decided it wants to accomplish. The chosen strategies cannot be mutually exclusive. For example, it may be quite difficult to have a strategy of being the leading technical innovator in an

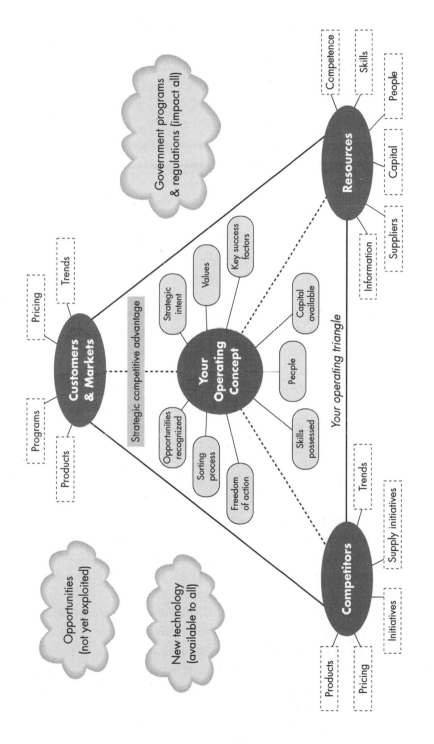

Figure 7.8: Strategy Creation Elements

industry and simultaneously be the lowest overall cost producer. Choosing randomly from a list of strategy options will not yield an integrated strategy set for the organization.

As was shown in Figure 7.6, strategies do not necessarily line up one for one with the objectives that have been set. For example, the organization may set an objective for economic return. Certainly the strategies for manufacturing, technical innovation, and customers and markets pursued will have a significant impact on meeting this economic objective.

After completing the strategies, it is always recommended to consider them in total. Will the organization be capable of implementing these strategies? Will the strategies work? If they are all completed successfully, will the organization accomplish its goals? How will the competition react to these strategies? Since these strategies will prescribe the actions that the organization is going to take, are they sufficient or are additional actions required?

It is always recommended to limit the number of strategies, since organizations are incapable of focusing on too many strategies simultaneously. So, while strategy number 56 may be outstanding, it will likely get lost in the shuffle. It is best to have between three and seven fundamental strategies. More than ten is usually too many.

Keeping that in mind, the intent is to add clarity and direction, so fewer is better only as long as the plan is complete. One vision, one mission, three to five objectives, one to five goals for each objective, three to seven strategies, and as many action plans as required to accomplish each strategy and ensure all goals are met—this starts to get fairly large. See Appendix B for forms and additional process hint information.

Initiatives and action plans. To implement the strategic plan and track its progress, a set of action plans, programs, or initiatives needs to be developed. The best approach for creating these action plans is to start with the strategies and ask what needs to be done to implement each strategy. It is best to start with near-term actions, and then consider actions further into the future. Responsibility for carrying out these action plans should be assigned and target dates for completion should be established. Follow-up on these action plans is a key method for the leaders of the organization to demonstrate that the strategic plan is an important procedure used in running the organization. In addition, it provides insight into which parts of the plan are working and which need added attention. A system for grouping these actions into a set of initiatives is discussed in detail in Chapter 10. The relationship of the four fundamental pillars of strategic planning is shown in Figure 7.9.

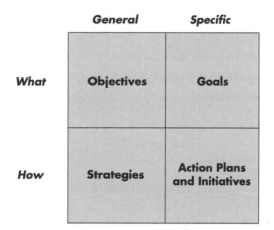

	General	**Specific**
What	Objectives	Goals
How	Strategies	Action Plans and Initiatives

Figure 7.9: The Relationship of the Fundamental Terms of Strategic Planning

The Endless Journey to the Vision

Strategic direction setting and action planning is a different way of working—it is not a temporary program or a task to be merely checked off the list.

This fundamental philosophy of the continuous improvement attitude is truly difficult for many to internalize, but it is critical for long-term competitive success. Since most organizations require some time to adapt to new

PERSPECTIVES

We have previously discussed team selection and size. The best creative strategy development projects that we have experienced were completed by small groups of three to seven people (and seven is sometimes too many). The group needs to simultaneously consider all the factors of the organizational direction, as well as those in the strategy creation elements model, and process the factors into meaningful creative approaches, all the while thinking in the future and contemplating possible system interactions. Using a strategy-creation facilitator is invaluable.

ways of operating, and they are not able
to move in giant steps, the time and
energy required should not be underestimated. The elements shown in the more

> *Strategic direction and alignment
> must be constantly improved.*

complete model of a strategic plan process in Figure 7.10 are constantly
changing and must be adapted into refinements to the strategic direction.
One should avoid the temptation to work on the elements without understanding the interactions. Understanding how the pieces fit together focuses
the analysis on what is important within and between each element.

Building Alignment

Strategic alignment principles are not limited to application in the board-
room. In fact, enlightened leaders have found that opportunities abound in
reducing organizational chaos, confusion, and conflict at all levels and in all
functions of organizations by using alignment techniques. In times of significant change, organizations are challenged to provide an approach to reeducate
the organization and to modify the culture to meet the newly defined direction. Rolling out a total organization alignment process (through planning),
along with lean management principles, is an excellent strategy to accomplish
this objective.

As organizations begin to align their assets they find that they derive
many benefits not only from the result, but also from the process of planning. Effective planning normally involves multifunctional groups of the top
managers of the organization. Since the process requires an open exchange
of ideas, concepts, values, and beliefs, a better understanding among the
managers usually results and the process is often cited as having tremendous
team-building effects. Communication is also improved as the dialogue
required to develop the plan results in a common understanding of what is
important and what is not. The values of the organization and of those who
do the planning become clearer, often resulting in improved working relationships within the work group. Truly effective organizations do not limit
this activity to the upper echelons. They involve multiple layers and levels
working on specific aspects of the plan or in creating their own subplan in
order to spread understanding and commitment as broadly as possible, as
shown in Figure 7.11. The creation of subplans is a wonderful way to
communicate and spread understanding of the real intent of the strategic

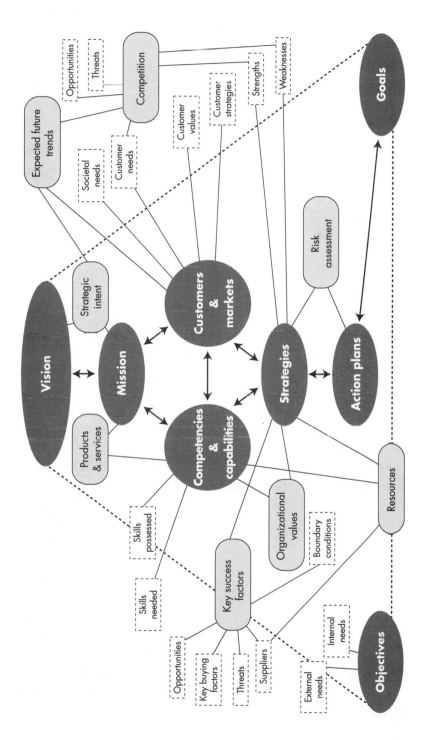

Figure 7.10: Strategic Plan Elements

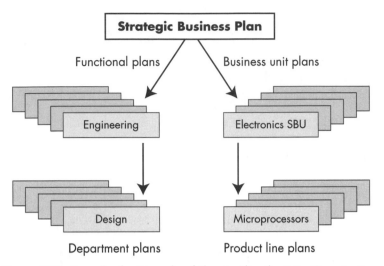

Figure 7.11: Example of a Hierarchy of Plans to Align the Entire Organization

direction throughout the organization. This provides a large part of the organization with an opportunity to participate and to be engaged in implementation.

Planning provides a common vision, and it defines the boundaries of the playing field. A better understanding of what is desired and what is required is created. This focuses the efforts of the organization, and it leads it toward achieving the vision. It also reveals when the organization is working on activities that are not within the defined boundaries. Through this it injects discipline (self-correction) into the organization.

When a well-designed planning process is spread across and cascaded down throughout the organization, improved communication, team-building, focus, and understanding of the vision usually result both horizontally and vertically. However, this is not enough to truly reduce the chaos of a totally reactive organization. In fact, the frustration level may increase if action does not accompany the plan, as more people understand what should be done. A plan without implementation is a wish. Therefore, a commitment to implementation should be part of any planning process. When plans are not implemented, many of the previously mentioned benefits resulting from the process of planning are lost as people become disenchanted with planning and disenchanted with the organization's ability to do what they now know needs to be done.

Staying On Track—The Challenge

A significant challenge is to stay on track in a dynamic environment. Change is continuous; therefore, plans must adapt with the world. The frequency of refreshing the plan is highly dependent on business and market conditions. In some businesses the refresh rate may almost need to be weekly, but the typical organizational timing is as follows once the plan is created:

- Every two years—complete reconstruction (rebuild with team input).
- Annually—complete refresh.
- Every six months—evaluate if any major changes of direction are needed.
- Monthly—complete staff status check of goal and action item progress.
- Continuously:
    - Address action item requirements and completion.
    - Monitor goal progress.
    - Observe for disruptive changes in the environment or market.

Sometimes the direction may need to be redefined due to significant market or business dynamics, but in most cases continuous improvement and course correction allow a more orderly and effective change. A particular challenge in many organizations is to stay on track when new managers or new management teams are installed. Organizations that have a well-established strategic direction find that having a clearly thought out and documented plan is invaluable in informing the new management about the business and its current strategy set.

Having a clear, documented plan in place that is widely understood provides a means to deal with transition when managers move to new positions. It not only aids the new manager, but also the people within the organization. The new manager can use the plan to understand the role of the group and its responsibilities to the overall plan. The people in the organization can continue to follow the plan while the new manager is moving up the learning curve. This facilitates the difficult transition period that occurs whenever managers change jobs.

Summary

Strategic planning is a complex activity that involves all parts of the organization. When it is carried out proactively with commitment, it will propel an organization out of a chaotic reactive state into a state where teamwork prevails, the focus is on winning, and everyone understands the part that they play. To say it simply, all of the assets will be aligned. In a truly lean organization, the content waste is minimized by reducing the effort being expended on activities that do not match with the strategic direction.

Once the strategic direction and management system is functioning as the way everyone does work rather than as an added activity, then progress will begin to accelerate without continuous management intervention.

The strategic plan chapter alignment of Figure 7.12 shows the basics of a strategic plan. The importance and impact of values were discussed in detail in Chapter 6. Additional details concerning metrics and goals are discussed in Chapter 8, and a process for implementation discipline is covered in Chapter 10.

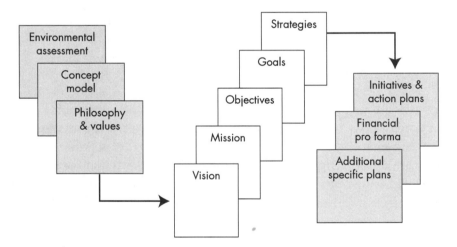

Figure 7.12: Strategic Plan Chapters

The process to create this type of plan can be successfully used to align an organization's people and systems, in order to focus it on accomplishing the desired outcomes. It uses proven methods to gain results in all aspects of a business or organization.

8

Deriving Metrics and Goals

Imagine going to a sporting event, say basketball, and not having a scoreboard. You do not know the score or the time remaining in the game. You do not know how many fouls have been committed or who committed them.

- *How exciting would it be for participants or fans?*
- *Do you think this approach would motivate players to perform their best?*
- *How would we know who was winning?*
- *How would the team decide when to slow the game down or call a time-out?*
- *Would anyone feel good about it?*
- *How many fans would be motivated to go to the game?*

Everybody knows this would not be much fun; however, many organizations operate without the benefit of keeping an accurate score. The majority of people want to be on a winning team and they need a scoreboard to know if and by how much they are winning. Goal tracking acts as the scoreboard for an organization.

The terms metrics and goals will be used in this discussion. Metrics are the measurement topics and goals are the specific targets (measure and timing). A growth metric might be sales revenue and the goal might be $300 million by the end of next year. Careful analysis should be used to determine both the metrics and the goals for organizations. Good metrics and goals:

- Quantify successful accomplishment of the business objectives.
- Provide information to support decision-making and help to manage value-creation.
- Drive the organization to work on the right things.

- Encourage the desired behavior.
- Drive individuals to do things the right way using the desired processes.
- Minimize gamesmanship and number manipulation.

Figure 8.1 shows the major process steps in deriving metrics and goals. Starting with the defined objectives, the first step is to brainstorm the list of possible metrics then distill this list through a filtering process.

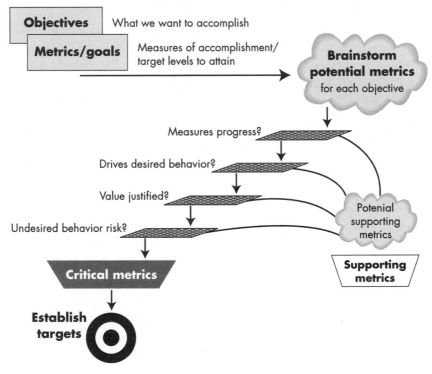

Figure 8.1: Metric and Goal-Setting Process

The major filters suggested are:

- Does the metric measure progress toward the vision and objectives?
- Will the metric drive the desired behavior and action?
- Does the process of getting and having the information add value? In this case, consider the true definition of adding value to customers and stockholders.
- How might the organization behave improperly as a result of this metric? Is the potential behavior risk manageable?

IN THE REAL WORLD

A client company was having difficulty in achieving its goals and asked us to perform a quick assessment of the situation and make recommendations. After some process sessions and interviews it was discovered that the management group had been convinced that sharing metrics and goals was imperative to achieving its targets. However, they had shared *all of their metrics* . . . totally confusing their workforce which was not familiar with this type of information.

An analogy to this situation may provide clarification. The pilot and the flight engineer on an airplane need to know what *all* the gages mean, but the flight attendants and passengers are only really interested in altitude, speed, and direction. In essence they only want to know that they are high enough so that they do not hit anything and that they are going fast enough in the right direction to arrive at their destination on time. Telling them about the readings on the other gages is not helpful.

Once the client company completed a lean assessment of its metrics and distilled them into a set of critical metrics that made sense to the workforce and to the managers, progress was made and workforce frustration dropped tremendously.

Key point: Everyone in the organization does not need all the information that the pilot has—the business pilot may be the CEO or the executive group. Great value results from keeping the key communicated organizational metrics simple, clear, and understandable—just like speed, altitude, and direction.

Additional questions and considerations in metrics development should include:

- Are there as few as possible to help the organization focus? (Think lean.)
- Do the metrics fit with the systems and culture of the organization?
- Do the metrics address results and process (behaviors)?
- Does the set make sense as a whole, and is it balanced across the various areas (finance, people, customers, etc.)?
- Keep the ideas that do not pass the filters, since they may be excellent supporting metrics that should be monitored (see Figure 8.2).
- Think lean and value-add—seriously evaluate those metrics that interfere with or misdirect the flow of value.

The key issue for organizational alignment is to define the goals and their level of priority. Many different methodologies have been used to create a hierarchy of goals. Whatever definitions are selected, they must be credible to the organization. The following list shows some of the names given to the various levels in potential goal hierarchies by an array of authors.

- Key focus goals:
  - Critical goals
  - Dash panel goals
  - Superordinate goals
- Supporting goals:
  - Guidance goals
  - Subordinate goals
  - Supporting goals
  - Subgoals
- Desired targets:
  - Stretch goals
  - Reach goals
  - "To Win" goals

It is easy to pick metrics and goals. It is extremely difficult to select the few key metrics (and goals—targets for the metrics) to drive organizational behavior in the desired direction and toward the strategic intent. Figure 8.2 shows the categorization of metrics, suggested by the authors, into three tiers:

- *Critical*—Metrics that provide critical performance information and drive desired behavior.

- *Guidance*—Metrics that provide guiding information but do not drive correct behavior by themselves.
- *Supporting*—Metrics that provide supporting, detailed information.

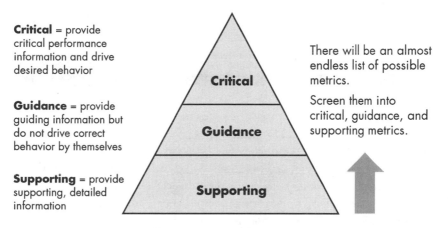

Critical = provide critical performance information and drive desired behavior

Guidance = provide guiding information but do not drive correct behavior by themselves

Supporting = provide supporting, detailed information

There will be an almost endless list of possible metrics.

Screen them into critical, guidance, and supporting metrics.

Figure 8.2: Filtering Categories for Brainstormed Metrics

Once the critical list of metrics is established, then, and only then, targets (goals) can be set for them. Target setting can be based on business needs, benchmarking, and a large array of other possibilities.

PERSPECTIVES

There are many excellent places to begin a crosscheck to ensure adequate coverage of the metrics arena (i.e., to reduce the risk of omitting valuable metrics): Quality System Certification requirements, Baldrige Award requirements, Appendix C of this book, and many other public domain references. The metrics from standard references may not fit the specifics of the organizational situation, or the cost to measure may far outweigh the value generated. Always ask, How will measuring this metric help us generate more value? True value-adding metrics are usually not difficult to measure once the business system is doing what it should be doing.

Key point: When objectives are carefully defined, the metrics (i.e., what should be measured) will roll directly from them.

It is important to decide the philosophy that will be used. Will the goals be minimum requirements, suggested performance hurdles, or almost unattainable goals? In mature organizations the goals are normally set as realistic high hurdles. The organizations that have tried setting minimum and expected goals usually end up on the low end of the performance spectrum (close to the minimum goal requirement).

NOTE

From our experience, we strongly suggest setting *realistically* high hurdles that are business- and customer-justified to drive realism into the need to accomplish the targets. Many goal-setting failures are derived from unrealistic and unfounded targets, which drive rational people to suspect management ineptitude and then divert their energy, creativity, and motivation away from goal accomplishment. Management credibility is critical for success when setting high-hurdle targets.

We also suggest that positive reinforcement, rather than punishment for lack of achievement, be used on high-hurdle goals. Deal with people who deliberately block progress as you would any other performance-deficient person.

If bonuses are in question and tied to metrics, then establish a system with thresholds that allow for greater bonus opportunity tied to higher performance achievement.

Hint: Make metric targets (goals) realistic and attainable with some stretch (i.e., do not make them too easy).

Excessive measurement can drive waste creation into the value stream. Therefore, it is necessary to focus efforts on metrics that help drive the flow of value. It may be helpful to view metric and goal establishment as a significantly iterative process that will benefit greatly from critical design reviews and potential failure-mode discussions. Some examples of metric intentions and risks (potential undesired consequences) are shown in Figure 8.3.

Beware of goal abuse. A good example is what is frequently called denominator management. That is where a goal is set as a ratio, and the ratio can be improved faster by lowering the denominator rather than by increasing the

Metric	Intentions	Risks
Development Time	• Improve speed to market • Lower engineering costs	• Eliminate/minimize development steps • Not count certain aspects (pre-development or productionization)
Sales $/Head	• Improve sales • Select projects with good return per engineer • Improve understanding of where resources are being used and efficiency of various projects	• Optimize sales without profit • Select "systems" programs over component programs • Cut strategic programs that have lower returns • Use as only decision indicator
100% On-time Production Launch	• Meet committed customer and internal production launch dates	• Set/agree to dates that are easily achievable that do not meet actual customer requirements
100% of Customer Commitments Met on Time	• Improve customer satisfaction • Improve market reputation	• Avoid commitments to difficult customer target dates • Negotiate dates to be more easily attained
Number of New Customer Programs	• Drive development of new products • Improve sales • Improve development time	• Take on programs to improve the number without regard to strategic needs or profit potential • Slice big programs into pieces to increase program count
Quality and Reliability	• Improve quality • Create market reputation	• Drive increased cost (focus on detection) • Overdesign/overtest products beyond customer needs • Overinvest and overresource programs
Number of New Products Launched	• Drive sales of new products and technologies	• Define products as different when in same family or technology group (not really new)
Number of Technology Benchmarks Completed	• Drive technology improvement and growth • Create new technological advances—creating competitive advantage	• Set and achieve benchmarks on technologies with little or no benefit to customers or market competitiveness • Benchmarks not truthful or relevant
Return on Net Assets (new product sales/net assets)	• Improve sales of new products versus the cost of the assets to achieve them	• Sell assets to reduce denominator
Budget Attainment	• Control costs to competitive and affordable levels	• No spending on required items to support goals/projects • Cost control overrides business logic and other goals
Break-even Time (time for profits to pay back development costs)	• Drive selection of projects to meet profit goals • Improve development process (cost and timing)	• Avoid longer term payback projects that may be strategic

Figure 8.3: Potential Metrics Impact

numerator. An example might be sales made as a percent of sales attempted. While the intent of this goal is to increase closed sales, it is clear that the ratio can rapidly be improved just by attempting to make fewer sales. If a salesman were successful early, he could relax and the real intent of the metric would be unrealized. This certainly is not the behavior that is wanted, but poorly conceived goals can easily lead to this type of behavior. If the intent of the goal is to increase sales closed, then the goal should be set as a specific number for

IN THE REAL WORLD

Total business thinking is required to make the trade-off decisions among goals. An extreme, but true, example will perhaps aid understanding. Several years ago we were working with a client in a developing nation where the cost of money was high (about 25 percent), unemployment was higher (about 40 percent), general production compensation was low (about $2 per hour), and in some cases common sense seemed to be missing altogether. In this environment our client organization had set its primary goals as eliminating production overtime and maximizing the products placed in finished goods inventory!! When a Pareto analysis of the company's costs was conducted, it was not surprising to find that inventory-carrying cost was their highest cost element and labor cost was their lowest cost element. Since the primary focus was on eliminating overtime compensation, our client was falling behind on customer orders for materials that were in finished goods inventory but required labor to package and ship! Blindly adhering to the two primary goals was causing our client significant customer dissatisfaction, loss of market share, and significant negative financial performance. Our client had missed the whole point of providing products to customers and getting paid for it. Instead the focus was no matter what, *do not work overtime*. By simply changing these two goals to more reasonable measures of performance, our client was able to significantly improve the financial situation.

The moral of this story is: Be careful when you set goals—your organization may blindly (or maliciously) follow them.

Key points: The entire goal set must be considered simultaneously (and in balance) and when the achievement of goals is hurting your organization, change them!

that variable based on research of what is currently being accomplished and what is required for future success.

⚠   Almost every possible metric has risks and can be abused when taken out of context. All of the risks shown in Figure 8.3 can be easily handled with good leadership and organizational understanding that the goals are to be considered as a total set and must all be balanced. Mature business thinking and mature business behavior are required to be effective and minimize wasteful activity in the arena of goal management. Frequent goal status reviews, at multiple organizational levels, provide an excellent forum for goal interpretation discussions and can be a very valuable tool in coaching the organization on business thinking.

Lean Metrics Example

An example for a typical business may help to solidify the concept further. Imagine that a large, global, business-to-business supplier of components and subsystems has developed its objectives, and they fall into the following categories:

1. Customers
2. Growth
3. People
4. Financial
5. Product
6. Production

These objectives have been processed into metrics, as shown in Figure 8.4.

In the example in Figure 8.4 the organization had 28 critical metrics; however, it had many more guidance and supporting metrics throughout the organization.

People always ask, How many goals should we have or how many is too many? The right number of goals is dependent on the quantity of objectives. It is highly suggested that the number of objectives be constrained to be less than seven, although some organizations operate quite successfully with as many as twelve. The right answer has more to do with the culture and ability of the organization to understand and balance the various forces of multiple objectives. One to five goals per objective is a very workable number at the high level, but guidance and supporting goals can provide the detail required

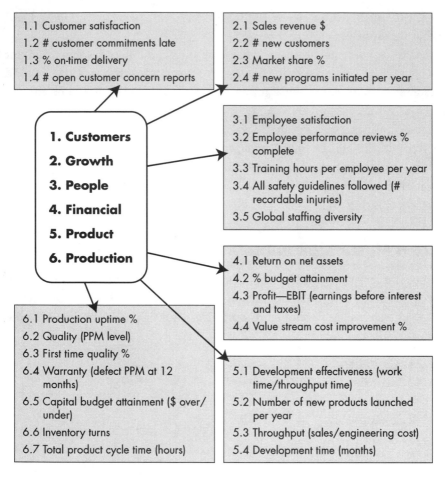

Figure 8.4: Example Metrics for an Organization

for other specific purposes. It may also be worthwhile to consider temporary metrics to deal with significant short-term or urgent issues, resisting the temptation to make them permanent. In summary:

- Fewer metrics are better.
- Keep metrics lean and simple.
- Keep the goals realistic to actual business requirements.

The desire is to have just enough goals to clearly define the targets and drive desired behavior—and no more. People try to accomplish those things to which management is paying attention, so providing clear targets is likely to get more of the right things accomplished.

PERSPECTIVES

Some of you may be concerned about not measuring all the detailed goals that are important. It has been our experience that, many times, when management focuses on the key measures and communicates the desired vision, multiple metrics show improved performance. Let us clarify. Many of the lesser metrics will also improve through a multitude of systemic interactions—which often almost seems like magic. Some of the sources that we have witnessed include:

- Interactions with the key metrics drive progress on lesser metrics.
- Secondary effects (interrelationships) move the lesser metrics.
- People resolve their issues before management discovers them now that they know management is paying attention and cares.
- Hawthorne effect—People see what management is seriously watching and begin to do their part.

In many cases metrics are measures of business processes that are inherently linked, so as the process performance improves, many of the metrics reflect this improvement. Understanding all of the interactions and relationships of the process and various metrics can be extremely difficult, if not impossible, in complex situations.

Key point: Focus management energy on improving performance of the higher order (critical) metrics and many of the secondary (guidance and supporting) metrics will be pulled up with them.

Goals Rolldown

Each division, department, group, function, and individual should link their goals to the high-level goals of the organization, as depicted in Figure 8.5.

Allowing people at each level to discuss and create (or suggest) their own goals is a wonderful technique for improving organizational alignment to the strategic intent. Care must be taken to do this properly, or it can result in time-consuming, wasteful activity. However, with proper facilitation and direction, these sessions can significantly improve the business thinking of the organization, align actions to the strategy, build a more common sense

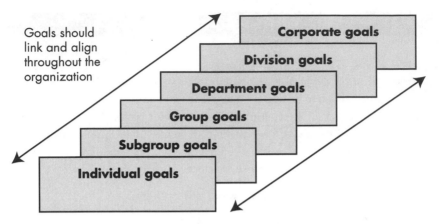

Figure 8.5: Goal Hierarchy

of purpose, and clarify the focus of the entire organization for many people who do not have the perspective to see it from their own positions.

Goals and Means

One of the major differences between American management by objectives and Japanese *hoshin* management is that every goal, or person who owns the goal, is provided with a means to accomplish the goal in the Japanese *hoshin* approach. In a Lean Management Systems approach, one is always concerned about both the results and the process (the means by which the results are obtained). Strategies should include the high-level means to accomplish the goals, and as will be described later in Chapter 10, action plans and initiative design should include a checkpoint to ensure that the process and action steps are capable of achieving the goals. In addition, the follow-up system must continue to address the question, "Is our process getting us to the desired results?"

Goals Visualization

One of the key aspects of lean is to simplify and clarify communications. Goal communication that is made visual is almost always more effective than words alone. The old adage that a picture is worth a thousand words applies in metric and goal communication as the example shown in Figure 8.6 demonstrates.

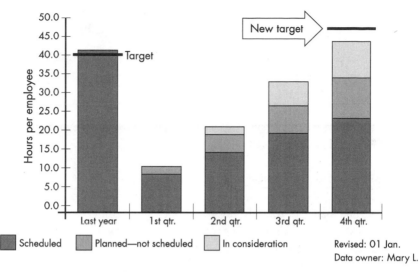

Figure 8.6: Visual Metric and Goal Communication Example

Showing goals visually provides the ability to see historical results, future targets, progress being made, and aspects of the detail (e.g., training hours scheduled). There are many possible visual metric and goal presentation styles. Selecting a style that is meaningful to the organization and is easily understood (i.e., not easily misunderstood) is recommended.

Summary

Visible goal progress measurement is one of the most powerful organizational motivation and organizational change tools available. How an organization keeps score drives a significant amount of the organizational action and behavior. A system evaluation of potential metrics—considering how they might work and how they might be misused—is highly recommended. Having great metrics and goals alone will not necessarily drive progress, but having goals along with implementation leadership can deliver tremendous progress.

The key points to remember about goals and metrics are:

- Set metrics and goals that drive the desired organizational behavior.
- Establish metrics and goals that add value to the organization's objectives.

- Link goals to customer and business requirements.
- Minimize the number of goals to allow focus.
- Make goal presentation visual and easily understandable.

Providing goals and measuring progress can allow more people to be winners (or to at least be more honest with where they really are)—generating creativity and motivation to accomplish even more.

A SPECIAL NOTE FOR LEAN LEADERS

We discussed setting realistic goals with some stretch as a general approach. For those leaders initiating a fully integrated lean approach, we suggest thinking in a nonlinear way about progress. Why should a group constrain its thinking to 10 percent improvement when 70 percent of its activity is waste? Why would it be unreasonable to set improvement targets to more than double performance? Many groups have experienced tremendous progress by striving for a two- to four-fold improvement.

We suggest using caution, as you may scare the improvement team into their proverbial foxholes and stifle all progress if you start with this type of "impossible" goal.

Suggestion: Educate the improvement team first and then walk them up the progress curve one step at a time at a speed that maintains the motivation of the team. Use the concept from the old proverb: The higher one climbs the more one can see.

9

Providing Process Structure

One of management's greatest gifts to the organization
is to provide processes and structure to accomplish
the objectives and goals.

Without clear processes, management does not get what is desired. Without clear processes, one usually gets organizational chaos. Without clear processes, management gets what it deserves. It is management's responsibility to ensure that processes exist to perform the required tasks. (Note: It is management's responsibility to see that such processes exist and that they work well—not that management must personally create them.)

The simple model that was shown in Figure 1.2 (page 5) indicates that strategy, structure, and process are all interrelated in a system. If given a clean slate, strategy would come first, then structure, and then process.

The optimum organizational design is for the structure to be optimized to the business direction and strategy. Very few are granted this situation; however, many are provided the opportunity to reconfigure the team structure or operating committee approach within the defined organizational structure. This can be a tremendous avenue for driving changes into both the system and the organizational mindset, when properly implemented.

Why do we need processes and policies? Basically we need processes to answer two questions:

- How do we do things around here?
- How do things work around here?

In the process arena, the challenge is to create just the right level of structure and discipline without stifling creativity and without adding too much bureaucracy. People adapt to the system of processes in which they exist. Increased throughput can be obtained by incrementally improving the process while leaving the major aspects relatively constant over the long term so the people in the organization can learn how to work in the system and can become more effective.

A simplified hierarchy of organizational processes is shown in Figure 9.1, starting with organizational direction and going through business approach, organizational structure, team structure, and ending with procedures and policies. This hierarchy should target answering the question, "How do things work around here?"

Direction
Business approach
Organizational structure
Team structure
Procedures and policies

Figure 9.1: Organizational Process Hierarchy

Aligning this process hierarchy with the strategic direction of the organization tremendously enhances the implementation of the strategic intent. The basic aspects are as follows:

- Strategy:
  - *Direction.* The strategic plan defines the direction and its implementation follow-up process.
  - *Business approach.* It is a combination of the philosophies and strategy of the organization.
- Structure:
  - *Organizational structure.* It is the visual hierarchy traditionally shown on organizational charts.
  - *Team structure.* If a team approach will be used, it can be defined much like the organizational structure to avoid confusion and conflict. A simplified example is shown in Figure 9.2.

- Process:
  - *Procedures and policies.* The procedures and policies define the processes, requirements, and guidelines for all of the organization's activities.

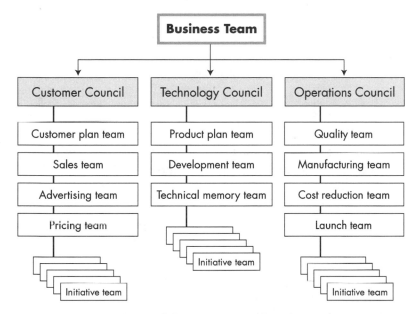

Figure 9.2: Team Structure Example

It is truly amazing how much more support organizations will provide when the direction makes sense and is consistent. Figure 9.3 shows the rollout from the strategic plan into the areas of:

- *Communication.* Actively decide what and how to communicate information to the organization.
- *Actions.* Clearly assign actions and develop a follow-up system to ensure appropriate organizational priority is given (see Chapter 10).
- *Procedures.* Define rules, policies, procedures, and processes consistent with the strategic direction.

Keep the rule set to an absolute minimum (lean) while defining all necessary requirements, so the organization does not waste time toiling on activities that will not meet the objectives and goals.

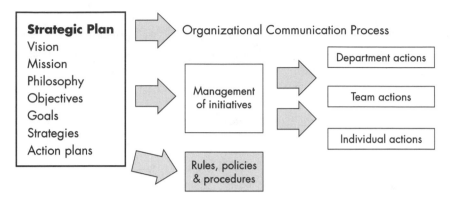

Figure 9.3: Strategic Plan Rollout

Experience indicates that having clarity on how to do things (especially when going through an organizational transition) is critical to maximize the motivation and the focus of the workforce. Driving everything to link with the strategic plan enhances coherence and support from the organization. Defining all the strategic work of the organization in the strategic plan, as shown in Figure 9.4, aligns the work of the management group and clarifies the desired priorities for the organization.

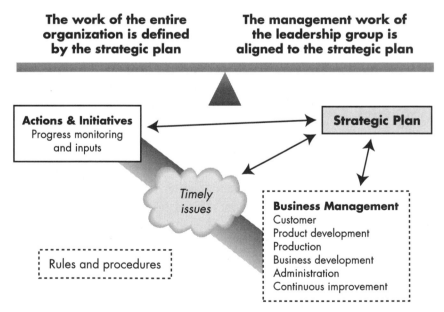

Figure 9.4: Strategic Direction Alignment

When designed in this manner, the agenda for frequent management staff strategy meetings becomes:

- Review initiatives and actions (select appropriate ones on a set schedule).
- Discuss timely issues (urgent and important unpredictable items).
- Cover communication issues (if not covered in other meetings).
- Perform any required reviews (operational, program, or status reviews).

Since the plan covers all the strategic aspects the management group should be managing, nothing is lost or forgotten, and it is simple to add new initiatives and action items as they arise. In this way, the system is constantly refreshed and up to date.

Cadence

To support staying on track and to further clarify organizational expectations, top management should define a cadence (the rhythm) for the organization. In Chapter 5, the concept of a management system diagram was introduced (and is repeated here in Figure 9.5). This process is an excellent methodology to build a cadence for the organization since it can be used at the various levels or layers of the organization. Actual experience in using the management system diagramming approach reveals several realities:

- It may be difficult to do the first iteration.
- Many enhancements and clarifications will occur over the first few months.
- Conflicts will become obvious (so they can be addressed).
- People will relax and begin to see how it all fits together.

Further clarity can be provided to the cadence by documenting the additional schedule-driven aspects of implementing the strategic intent and accomplishing the goals and action items. For example, defining the yearly schedule for a business team running a sector of a business will align the organization to prepare accordingly, and on time, for the requirements of the management agenda, thus driving implementation of the defined strategic intent.

While documenting the management system can appear to be simply added paperwork, the benefits that are realized far exceed the effort required.

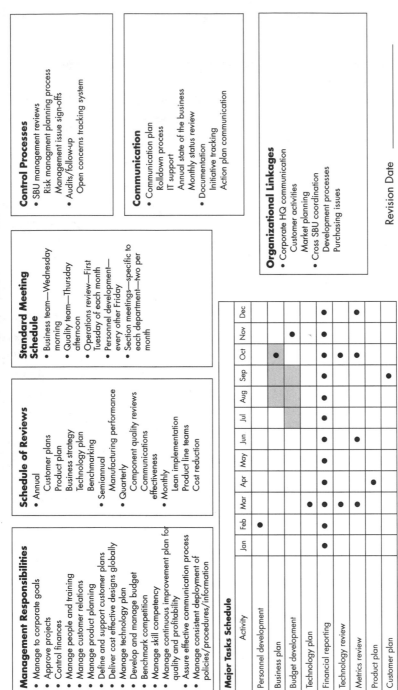

Figure 9.5: Management System Diagram Example

It has been shown repeatedly that it saves tremendous organizational waste to clearly define the approach and process. Doing this once in the beginning prevents the need for the organization to do it many times later, at each point of issue.

IN THE REAL WORLD

When the management system diagram is effectively completed, the appropriate management teams, meeting structure, and schedule become clear and improvements can be easily developed. Selecting the appropriate decision-making processes and meeting structure is the main goal of the management system design activity. Far be it for us to suggest creating a bureaucratic meeting structure that does not add value. In fact, the meeting structure can be a significant source of waste. However, the complete lack of a structure has the high potential to create unrecognized waste through ad hoc, uncoordinated processes.

Several years ago, while working with a European client, we helped design the management system and cadence required to keep everything moving smoothly. One of the members of management was dead set against creating a team that would meet in a structured system to carry out its tasks. His reasoning was that he was busy meeting individually with each of the people who would be on the team already and did not have time to add a regular meeting on top of the ad hoc meetings he was already having. It was amusing that he was unable to recognize that if he had regular scheduled meetings, all the ad hoc meetings would not be required. He would actually have more time and the organization would be more aligned, as they would all hear the same thing at the same time and be able to dialogue for clarification. One day, while discussing this with him in the hallway, we were interrupted by one of these ad hoc meetings. Our management friend turned to us and said, "See what I mean. There just isn't time to add your structured meetings on top of all these meetings that I need to be able to get my job done." We are not sure that our client friend ever truly recognized the value of the structured versus ad hoc meeting approach. However, the CEO did recognize the value and continued to work with his organization until they also could see how the applied structure could make the organization better. He then implemented the system.

PERSPECTIVES

Perhaps it should not need to be said—however, time and again we have experienced organizations in a change process that seemed to forget to engineer the new process before shutting down the old one. This is much like a couple with six children deciding they need more room and bulldozing their house to build a new one without arranging for a place to stay in the interim—and then it begins to rain. Multimillion-dollar operations can virtually be brought to a standstill for months when careful planning is not implemented. Many people attach their comfort and capability to a long-established organizational structure and/or process. This can be both good and bad—either way it needs to be recognized. Designing the new process so that it adds value and makes sense to the organization is required. Having a step-by-step conversion plan will reduce waste in making the transition from the old process and provide smoother implementation.

Process Discipline

Figure 9.6 shows the importance of implementing in a way that optimizes the results through careful management of the discipline level. Structure and process are good to a point, but the old adage, "too much of a good thing," also applies here. Highly creative and motivated people need to have some flexibility and space to use their thinking abilities.

Organizations need to balance the drive for common processes with the drive for creative process improvement. Once people truly understand the concepts of lean, value add, and waste, the logic for these discussions becomes much clearer. Until this threshold is reached, having a lean coach in the discussion group helps bring clarity to the issues and decisions.

Clear, High Quality Checkpoint Reviews

The key concept of the previously discussed process is to build organizational coherence through group reviews and communication. This assumes that the organization has processes and has checkpoint reviews that are of high quality. This may seem inherently obvious, but it is not obvious in organizational

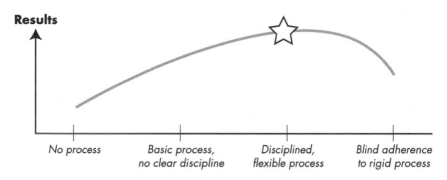

Figure 9.6: Process Discipline Optimization Leads to Results

practice. Many organizations have processes that are not much more than giving themselves a checkmark for making any attempt at following the process. This approach will not yield adequate results. Tough go/no-go decision requirements, quality work, and critical reviews by people who have the benefit of organizational learning are expected in these management checkpoint reviews.

One must remember, the purpose of these reviews is to improve understanding of all people attending (i.e., communication), to improve the approach (i.e., strategy quality), and to improve the results through critical review and discussion by experienced people. A significant positive side effect is that this approach develops subordinates and reaffirms the review process as part of the expected culture.

How Does One Improve Business Processes?

There are many tools and techniques for improving business processes that have been mentioned and they are further discussed in Chapter 11. It is very desirable to use standard approaches and terminology across the organization. However, many organizations have caused tremendous havoc and organizational disruption by decreeing that only a standard set of techniques (or one technique) may be used. Creative people need flexibility and the ability to have an input into what may become the standard process of tomorrow. Management should carefully move toward standardized approaches, yet be flexible enough to try new concepts. This dichotomy requires insightful consideration, and defined approaches for analyzing and testing new concepts. It is much easier to command everyone to follow the standard processes than it is to evaluate whether these processes are stifling creativity. Virtually any process can be improved. However, when the process is in place and working well, one should be careful when tinkering with it in the name of creating flexibility. It is another one of those balancing situations that must be faced in directing an organization.

Process Analysis Example

One of the major techniques for business improvement is flow analysis (also see Appendix D for detailed information on flow analysis). The traditional approach to process analysis is to create a flowchart of the process and then to find ways to improve the flow. Many new twists have been taken on this fundamental concept under many names—flow analysis, value analysis, value stream mapping, value mapping, process blueprinting, flow evaluation, serv-

---

NOTE

We are certain that someone will ask the question, "How do we tell what is flexible and what is not?" Here is the interesting irony regarding flexibility of processes. In the short term, nothing is flexible, and in the long term, everything is flexible. The attitude of the organization should be that once a process is established, it must be followed. However, every process can be improved, and it is everyone's responsibility to propose ideas for improvement. If this philosophy is followed, answering the flexibility question becomes a moot point. To avoid anarchy when it comes to improving processes, it is strongly recommended that a process for suggesting, validating, approving, and implementing new processes be consciously developed, clearly communicated, and rigorously followed.

Key point: We should constantly strive to improve all processes, but all processes are inflexible until we agree to change to the new, improved approach. In other words, the flexibility comes from the *opportunity* to improve the process, not from changing any process at any time.

---

ice blueprinting, lead-time reduction, continuous process improvement, process reengineering, etc.—each with their specific uniqueness. However, the key concepts are the same:

- Understand the steps in the process.
- Measure performance criteria of the steps.
- Brainstorm improvements.
- Improve.

A more complete process flow is shown in Figure 9.7.

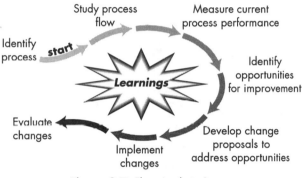

Figure 9.7: Flow Analysis Steps

It is highly recommended that the organization select one terminology (and process methodology) and stick with it to minimize organizational confusion and communication challenges.

The first step is to have a process, or at least a limited number of possible processes from which one can be distilled. The lean implementation specialist should then make certain the process fits into the macro business system. If it does not fit, it should be eliminated. If it does fit, then it should be improved. A helpful technique to create conceptual understanding includes creating a flowchart of the current process, creating an ideal lean-state process, and then distilling a desired process that will be implemented.

A simple example may illustrate the point of how waste exists in evolved business processes and how it can be reduced by process improvement techniques. Figures 9.8a, 9.8b, and 9.8c show an analysis of an expense reimbursement process with a current state, an ideal lean state, and a desired future state. Many companies have very detailed travel and individual expense reporting and processing systems. These systems have evolved over the years so that often a very complex, time-consuming report format has been created to facilitate data entry and data reporting by a functional support organization. Figure 9.9 summarizes the metrics and results from the analysis in Figures 9.8a, b, and c.

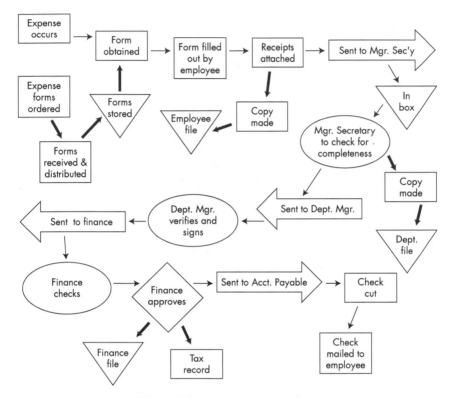

Figure 9.8.a: Current State Analysis

The analysis in Figure 9.9 shows reducing the process lead time from 55.5 days to 7.5 days and reducing the equivalent cost of managing expense reports from $375 to $75 per expense report. Careful analysis and consideration of the relative value of time spent on the specific tasks provides insight into optimizing the process value.

Within the fundamental management system of most organizations, there are numerous examples where systems are not optimized or are optimized around a relatively inexpensive resource while wasting expensive resources. The lean process improvement techniques provide an approach to remove the waste and provide increased value.

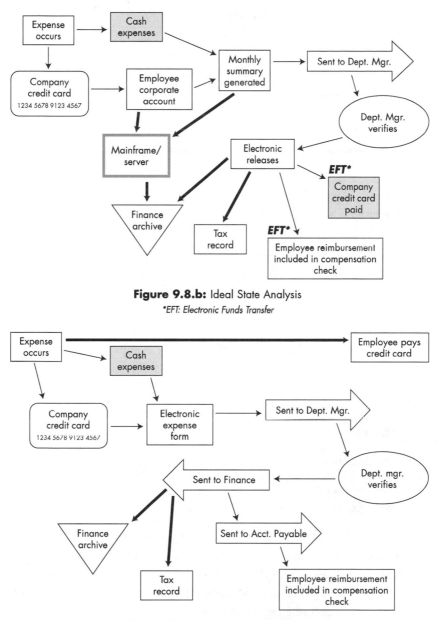

Figure 9.8.b: Ideal State Analysis
EFT: Electronic Funds Transfer

Figure 9.8.c: Desired State Analysis

The insightful lean improvement specialist would remind us that, in our example, the entire expense report process provides no customer value and provides no value to corporate assets. Certainly, parts of it can provide a risk

Metrics Summary

Step		Lead time (days)		
		Current	Ideal	Desired
1	Fill out initial forms	1.5	0.0	0.3
2	In secretarial process	6.0	0.0	0.0
3	Manager approval	6.0	0.3	1.2
4	In Finance process	15.0	0.3	3.0
5	At Accounts Payable	12.0	0.0	3.0
6	Check in process to employee	15.0	0.0	0.0
Total lead time (days)		55.5	0.6	7.5
Total number of people required to manage the system		5	2	4
Paper copies in the system		4	0	0
Cost ($)/claim		375	35	75

Figure 9.9: Metrics Summary

mitigation of tax accounting issues. There is still room for improvement and, in the example above, the process still costs $75 each. It is amazing how scraping away waste exposes more waste once one knows what it is and how to look for it.

Summary

Clear process structure defines:

- How we do things.
- How the system works.

Defining clear processes and procedures is a key step toward becoming lean. Aligning the system to be consistent with the strategic direction directly enhances the successful implementation of the defined strategic intent. Individuals in the organization that understand the rules, the system, and how they fit into it, perform better and deliver results.

IN THE REAL WORLD

The power of applying these techniques is reinforced to us when we work on problems with clients. We were working with an American client who had a requisition approval process that was restricting the completion of projects and slowing down the manufacturing operations. Each person of the management staff recognized it as a cross-functional process, but knew that the problems resulted from the other function's stubborn refusal to follow the system, even if it was slow and cumbersome. As we attempted to help them map the high-level process (essentially model the cross-functional interaction relationship) it became clear that there was a disconnect as to what the true process was or was supposed to be. Everyone had a different opinion about what was and was not supposed to happen.

A detailed process flow analysis was started, and very quickly the group was logjammed at the third step, which happened to be a communication activity. After a few minutes of passionate discussion, we realized that there were at least two approaches to the process functioning in a distinctly different way. We asked the team to define their customers and suppliers from the preceding and following steps of their respective activity, and sent them out to get a sample of every form that is either received or supplied. Amazingly, as each person presented their documents, the process grew and grew in complexity. When the analysis was complete, 18 different documents for doing essentially the same thing were identified, with five major process flows identified through which these various documents controlled the value stream. This, of course, shocked the group, and was surprising to us as well, especially when one of the processes was a covert approach to bypass process rules and skip over at least two functional control points. Everyone was trying to do what they thought was the right thing in a different way.

The power of the process analysis and the alignment discussions they generated was tremendous. This particular analysis activity resulted in two redesigned processes (a standard flow and an expedited flow) that required only three documents—down from five processes and 18 documents.

10

Discipline and Relentless Follow-up

Progress occurs only when action is taken.

Discipline in implementation is the key to getting things done. A structured approach at first seems to require more work than the traditional approaches used in many organizations. This is because it requires extra effort to create a structured implementation system and, in the beginning, this is work on top of the work that is already being done. However, organizations usually find that once a system is implemented, this investment helps them to accomplish more and reduces the overall workload. Implementation systems can range from a simple action plan list that is tracked on a frequent basis, to a complete organizational rolldown of detailed initiatives and actions for every individual that is monitored instantaneously on a computer-based system. Most organizations find that something in between is most effective from a cost and value-adding perspective.

Leadership theorem:
People work on what
management watches.

One of the key insights into getting things done is to make tasks, and the status of task progress, a matter of public record within the organization. Most organizations do this as a matter of course in production or service areas, posting measures of production output, quality, number of customer orders processed, number of customer complaints, etc. Yet, this tactic is not easily visible in most administrative areas.

Publicly tracking conformance to strategic (critical and high level) action plan requirements for employees and top managers alike can drive great results. It is amazing how public exposure:

- Drives achievement of actions (through peer pressure and competition).
- Drives other people to support the action accomplishment.
- Builds a better business understanding throughout the organization.

Letting the entire organization know what is on the top of management's priority list can be a great process for further aligning the entire organization to implement the strategic intent of the organization. It is extremely important to consider carefully what information to present publicly—that is, to all employees. Acquisition, alliance, personnel, competitor, and other sensitive initiatives and action plans should be securely presented in a controlled manner (or held as confidential).

Action Plan Tracking

There are many approaches for tracking performance and action items. The amount of detail to document and systematize should be decided based on the culture of the organization, the rate of change in the market, the rate of change in the organization, the size of the organization, the geographic dispersion of the organization, and the level of complexity of the action items.

For small organizations, a relatively simple action item list with priority, due dates, and the responsible persons may suffice to track performance and require minimum wasteful effort. This list may only need to be reviewed weekly or monthly, depending on the level of detail. The old saying "There is magic in the pen" (see Figure 10.1) is certainly true when applied to getting action items accomplished through systematic tracking.

Very large and dispersed organizations may want to track thousands of actions through the use of commercial or custom software applications. For high-technology firms, this may fit right into the culture and be easily accomplished, but for others, there is a great risk of tremendous bureaucracy and computer system logjams that can severely limit progress.

The purpose of tracking action items is to improve the effectiveness and efficiency of getting them accomplished. If the system does not do this, then it is wasteful and needs to be rethought, adjusted, or reconfigured. A very

There is magic in the pen

Writing it on paper

– *Clarifies your thinking*

– *Allows for increased communciation and understanding*

– *Creates a solid foundation from which to learn and make progress*

Figure 10.1: The Power of Documenting

effective way to accomplish action item tracking, focus on metrics and goals, and create a clear understanding for the organization is to create a publicly communicated initiative system that is linked to the strategic intent of the organization. The remainder of this chapter describes this approach.

Strategic Initiative Systems

Figure 10.2 shows the linkage of planning processes, the strategic plan itself, and the initiative implementation process that answers the question, "How will we make sure we make progress?"

This type of initiative system approach has been successfully used at many companies and organizations and is conceptually based on learnings from management by objectives (MBO) and *hoshin kanri* (*hoshin* management)— successfully used by Toyota and other Japanese firms.

Most organizations that invest time in strategic planning and understanding their management system create a plethora of strategic action items. The strategic initiative system described here merely categorizes these actions into natural groupings around the strategies, so they may be managed in an integrated and efficient manner. The two proven successful methods for creating initiatives are based on deterministic and free-flow approaches. The deterministic method is to start with the strategies and create the list of major initiatives required to implement each strategy and then develop the specific actions within each initiative. The free-flow method is to creatively brainstorm all the ideas for actions to implement the strategies and then to sort them into natural groupings, which then become initiatives.

IN THE REAL WORLD

We constantly caution our clients to beware of offsetting the benefits of tracking action items with the bureaucracy that creates significant waste on input and tracking. This caution comes from experiencing organizations that have invested significant amounts of money in large bureaucratic systems that do not work effectively. One such organization actually spent in excess of $1 million on tracking software that was intended to track all sales call figures as well as a database of all customer problems and improvement ideas. There were literally thousands of ideas that required tracking. The input and management cost for this system was approximately $200,000 per month. This moderate-sized organization was soon buried in tasks to feed the system. In spite of the fact that the system was not generating benefits greater than the cost, the organization was forced to use the system because of the large sunk cost. Finally, this system collapsed due to the unwillingness of people to "feed" and manage it.

We strongly believe in analyzing the cost benefit of any system, and realistically considering what it will take to make the system work efficiently along with how the output of the system will be used. This type of assessment can be completed using lean concepts to keep the value add high. Our casual observation is that the larger and the more ambitious a system is, the more likely it is to fall short in meeting its stated goals.

Key point: Implementing lean concepts at the onset of the system design could have averted tremendous organizational waste and pain. Lean is focused on doing the work in a way that adds the highest value. In many cases, relatively simple visual systems, when properly designed, work extremely well, adapt easily, meet speed requirements, and have very low maintenance costs. In addition, they are flexible, allowing the system to be adjusted without a massive rework.

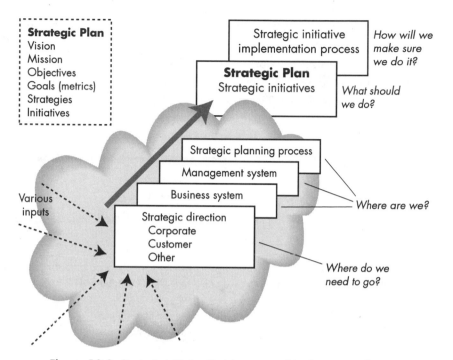

Figure 10.2: Strategic Initiative Development and Implementation Process

Remember, the purpose of the initiative system is to focus the efforts of the organization on implementing the strategies and accomplishing the goals. When tracking the effectiveness of the initiatives, a good approach is to ask the question: "When we have completed these initiatives, will we accomplish the goals in our plan?" If the answer to this question is no, then some added actions or initiatives may need to be generated.

An example for a typical business may help to solidify the concept further. A large, global, business-to-business supplier of components and subsystems has developed its strategies, and they fall into the following categories:

1. Customer satisfaction
2. Global growth and profitability
3. People development
4. Technology
5. Quality
6. Product development
7. Production
8. Operating systems

From these the organization develops the required initiatives shown in Figure 10.3. Caution should be exercised to establish enough initiatives to adequately cover all the strategic work of the organization for the next planning period, but also not to overload the organization with so many initiatives that nothing can be accomplished. The right number depends on the organization and its culture—but 20 to 50 initiatives are typical. The number of initiatives

Figure 10.3: Strategies and Strategic Initiatives Example

The initiative system drives detailed responsibility and ownership throughout the organization

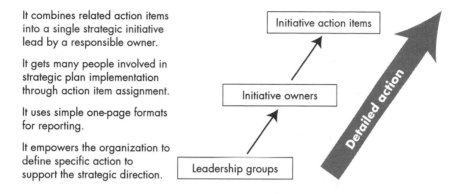

It combines related action items into a single strategic initiative lead by a responsible owner.

It gets many people involved in strategic plan implementation through action item assignment.

It uses simple one-page formats for reporting.

It empowers the organization to define specific action to support the strategic direction.

Figure 10.4: Broad Organizational Involvement Improves Alignment

depends on many factors, including diversity of the business, geographic spread of the operations, level of detail desired by the organization, and how the organization chooses to design the work.

Initiatives require an owner (or champion) and may require a small working team. Initiative owners are usually managers and supervisors. However, action item owners should encompass the entire organization to gain further organizational learning and involvement. Figure 10.4 shows this concept of total organizational involvement and the resulting improvement in alignment.

Initiatives can be documented in various ways, but the simple-looking format in Figure 10.5 and the completed form in Figure 10.6 show a very functional approach that has been successfully implemented. This initiative to reduce costs fits as a subinitiative under # 2.5 Profitability Management, shown in Figure 10.3. The formats are simple to use, but only after the organization gains some experience in working with them. Note that the initiative is linked to the strategic plan strategies and the strategic plan goals to keep everything aligned with the high-level direction.

It is important to ensure that all strategic plan goals that require improvement actions are covered by an initiative (see upper right-hand corner of the format in Figure 10.5). If not, it may be necessary to consider additional initiatives or an initiative to simply track all goal progress, and drive any additional required actions.

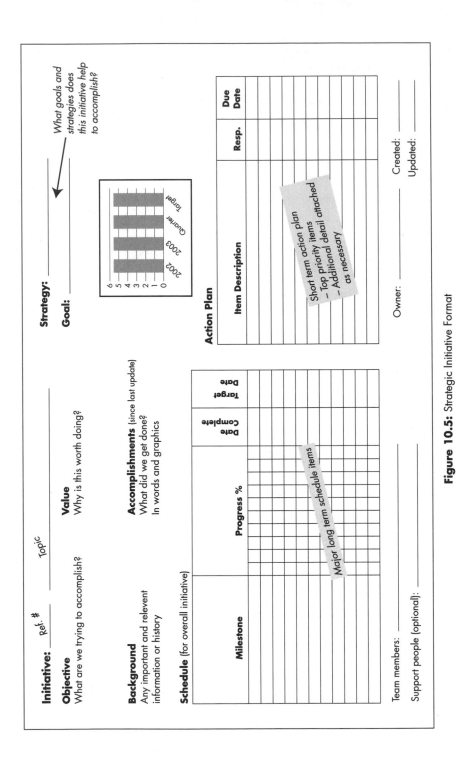

Figure 10.5: Strategic Initiative Format

Initiative: 77   Reduce cost   **Strategy:** 2, 3

Value Example

Goal: 1.2, 2.4

Objective
- Develop and implement overall action plan to reduce cost in production and administration areas

Value
- Company survival and prosperity
- Improved profitability
- $1,000,000 savings target per year

Cost Reduction ($000)

Background
- We are losing competitiveness against our key competitors

Accomplishments (since last update)
- Lean activity started in production cell #3
- Purchasing reduced price of gadgets from supplier 23 by 6 percent

Schedule (for overall initiative)

Milestone	Progress %	Date Complete	Target Date
Reduce widget cost by 5%		7/15/03	8/15/03
Lean activity—cell 2		6/27/03	7/1/03
Lean activity—cell 3			9/1/03
Lean activity in engineering			9/1/03
Lean activity—cell 7			10/1/03
Close dept. 22 and 43			10/1/03
Redesign shipping and receiving			10/15/03
Lean activity—cell 4			11/1/03
Exit production of old parts			11/15/03
Plan for next improvement cycle			12/1/03
Get management approval of plan			12/15/03

Action Plan

	Item Description	Resp.	Due Date
1	Start lean work in cell 7	Joe	8/15/03
2	Create improvement team in engineering	Mary	7/1/03
3	Purchase new punch press	Larry	9/1/03
4	Install new computer in cell 6	Gary	9/1/03
5	Redesign machine #33	Karen	10/1/03
6	Submit capital request for cell 4	Jack	10/1/03
7	Find new supplier for part 2004	Jim	11/1/03
8			11/15/03
9			12/1/03
10			12/15/03

Team members: Sally Jones, Sam Washington

Support people (optional):

Owner: Joe Smith   Created: 1/16/03

Updated: 7/25/03

Figure 10.6: Strategic Initiative Example

These one-page formats are based on the successful Toyota process for a one-page story, sometimes called an A3 report—A3 being the size of paper on which they were traditionally created. This concept has been used at various times in numerous American companies

"The things which matter most must never be at the mercy of things which matter least."

Johann Wolfgang von Goethe— German Writer (1749–1832)

as well. The one-page format requires that the entire story be totally visible on the one page to minimize non-value-added content and to assure that the entire story can be seen by all — with nothing being hidden in a thick report.

Initiatives can be further broken down into subinitiatives if required, as shown in Figure 10.7. However, the intent is to keep the master initiative as a one-page story that is coherent on its own. The one-page story concept can require small fonts from time to time, but the intent should be to tell the story graphically and to include only the important parts in the story, rather than just using smaller font sizes. The one-page concept forces a logical, clear presentation. This also weeds out the non-value-adding content and may be difficult (at first) for some organizations that are accustomed to long, detailed reports. Multiple pages may be used, however, when absolutely required for detailed support—with each page being a one-page story.

A lean approach means taking the waste out, and the initiative system is designed to reduce waste. The approach should be tailored to meet the organization's specific situation and specific needs. The formats are not critical—the thinking is critical. Therefore, one should adapt the formats to meet the needs of the organization. The cascading to subinitiatives shown in Figure 10.7 is an

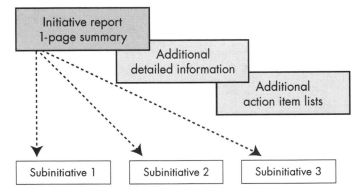

Figure 10.7: Initiatives and Subinitiatives

extremely effective way to involve more people in the implementation of the organization's strategic intent.

Managing Strategic Initiatives

The set of strategic initiatives should be managed in a way that further builds the organizational culture desired. Figure 10.8 highlights a few considerations including, initiatives should define all the strategic work of the organization, they should be the way work is done, and they should be the way progress is managed.

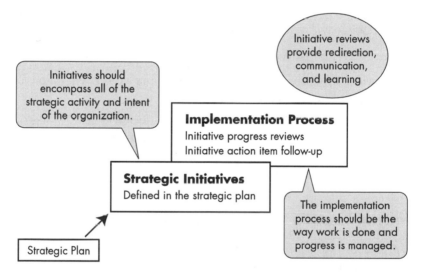

Figure 10.8: Strategic Initiative Implementation Process

In addition, the implementation of these initiatives can be more effective if:

- Initiative reviews are scheduled with a planned cadence.
- Initiatives are reviewed on the frequency required to maintain appropriate priority (weekly, monthly, or quarterly).
- Initiative summaries (except confidential ones) are posted for communication and visual management—visual responsibility posting also drives performance.
- Initiatives are assigned to various people for developmental exposure or to test their ability.
- Actions within initiatives cover a broad scope of the organization.

- Initiatives are both short term and long term.
- New initiatives are added as required within the context of the strategic intent of the organization.
- Initiative owners with unacceptable performance are, at first, given support to achieve the required performance level, and replaced if the unexceptional performance persists.
- Initiatives drive subteams or subinitiatives to broaden organizational participation.
- Significant initiatives or groups of initiatives are coordinated by a council; for example, the product plan, technology plan, and competence plan initiatives might be coordinated under the watchful eye of a technology council.

The strategic initiative process:

- Provides structure, process, visualization, and action item follow-up.
- Enhances business thinking.
- Promotes rational approaches and actions throughout the organization.
- Provides a logical approach to manage and control the business.
- When properly implemented, this process aligns the organization and facilitates accomplishment of the defined goals and actions.

Communication and Visual Management

Boss pressure drives urgency, but peer pressure drives progress. The most successful action item tracking systems visually show progress on action item accomplishment with the associated due dates and responsible parties. By publicly (within the organization) posting the tracking system, it can show at a glance where progress is being made and where it is lagging, thus identifying where the problem areas are located so that extra focus can be given. It can also create healthy competition within the organization. The following list of possible communication modes applies to actions or initiatives:

- Posting on a communication board.
- Posting in a controlled conference room (i.e., a war room or planning center).
- Posting on a controlled access local server (i.e., electronic storage).
- Communicated weekly in staff meetings with electronic or paper handouts.

Making the tracking visual and public helps to align the organization and gets more of the organization helping the action item owners, who may be at risk of missing the due dates.

Commitment

Commitment to the process is a requirement for successful implementation, and for the initiative system to work, top managers must be absolutely committed to working with it and then sticking with it. Starting this process and then dropping it can cause severe loss of management credibility.

IN THE REAL WORLD

Several years ago we worked with a European client in helping them establish and implement their strategic intent. We introduced an initiative management system for the entire enterprise similar to the one described in this chapter. One of the members of the management team with whom we worked was so impressed with the initiative management system for the enterprise that he asked if we would help him create a similar system for his functional department. We assisted him in creating a similar system for his engineering function, and he was able to significantly improve the direction and throughput for his department. This yielded a one-page project management tool. When a member of the sales organization from their United States subsidiary became aware of this system, he asked for assistance in creating a similar system for tracking sales initiatives. This yielded a one-page strategic customer-planning tool. In both cases, enlightened managers recognized the value in another application of a tool that would help the performance of their specific departments. The power of the one-page report process can be applied in many arenas, creating tremendous value and reducing waste.

Key points: The application of tools will usually be more successful when there is a pull rather than a push to cause them to be implemented. Also many of the Lean Management System techniques can be easily modified to meet the specific needs of the exact situation.

Top management must hold themselves and others accountable to stay on the course and stay with the process for an adequate period of time to instill the new way as *the* way business will be done. This typically means two to five planning cycles. This persistence is required in any approach to change an organizational system.

Summary

Discipline and relentless follow-up are required to drive progress and to keep progress moving until the new system becomes the norm in the organization. Action item management is the simplest and the most ignored avenue for making progress in organizations. A strategic initiative management system has been presented with its many benefits. Careful attention should be given to the design of the follow-up system to ensure it:

- Aligns the organization.
- Supports the culture (or cultural change) desired.
- Drives timely accomplishment of the actions.

Many organizations experience some frustration in the early implementation of follow-up systems. Rest assured that the organization will get better with practice. It is critical that patience and perseverance prevail. Involving the key managers in the design and implementation of a robust initiative system has proven to help organizations to stay the course and to stay on course, even during challenging times. Therefore, organizations need to have both a system for action plan management and the discipline to relentlessly follow-up to ensure success.

11

Technique Selection
and Application

*Selecting the right few things to do and managing them
in an integrated manner is critical to successful implementation
of strategic intent and Lean Management Systems.*

Up to this point, 10 chapters of philosophies, processes, approaches, and stories about strategic intent, leadership, lean management, and metrics, along with a plethora of other supporting information have been presented. What follows is the difficult challenge of choosing the right technique, at the right time, and with the right style of implementation.

The selection of the appropriate technique and application is very much like putting together a jigsaw puzzle—with the additional challenges that there are no straight edges to provide a frame, some of the pieces may be missing, and there is no box cover to provide guidance. Each organizational situation can be its own unique puzzle to be solved, as represented in Figure 11.1.

Everyone reaches a point in solving a jigsaw puzzle where the subject begins to take shape and the result becomes clear. All that is left is to find the remaining pieces that fit within the gaps. Puzzle pieces, that at one time had no meaning individually, very quickly complete the overall picture. Equally, when selecting the set of techniques for an organization, the pieces necessarily need to fit together as an integrated set that completes the desired picture. Technique selection is an area where rigorous analysis, systems thinking, and careful planning, combined with experience and clear thinking, will provide insightful guidance.

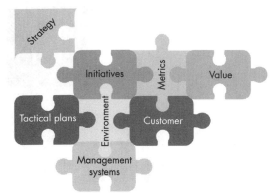

What is the picture (vision)?

Where are edges (boundaries)?

Where might we start (priority)?

Figure 11.1: Technique Selection Is Like a Puzzle

NOTE

Answering the question, "Which tools and techniques should you use?" is like trying to answer the question, "How do you cook anything?" Of course there is no single answer to this food preparation question. It depends on what you are trying to cook, and the desired attributes of a particular dish. To illustrate, we could say, "Always boil water and place the food item in it," but that would not work very well if the intent were to have fried eggs! Have you ever tried to fry a hard-boiled egg? It can be done, but the results will not yield what was expected. There is no *simple*, fuzzy logic or process that will yield the 100% correct answer of which technique should be used. The question of which techniques to use is a significant problem for many organizations since there are so many programs, so many techniques, and so much marketing hype around them.

The subject of technique selection must be addressed with this caution in mind: Thinking is required, and experience is a great teacher.

The process for selecting appropriate techniques can be quite complex. In a simplified view, the major steps in determining which techniques best fit the organizational needs are to:

1. Assess the situation.

2. Confirm or establish the strategic direction.

3. Select Lean Management Systems techniques.

4. Implement.

5. Learn and improve.

To build upon this simplified model, the following areas are each addressed in more detail in the sections that follow:

- Assessment techniques—how to assess the situation.
- Strategic direction-setting techniques—how to set strategic direction.
- Lean Management Systems techniques—how to implement Lean Management Systems.
- Systemic and priority considerations—how to consider system impacts and how to balance long- and short-term opportunities.
- Technique selection process—how to select appropriate techniques.
- Technique implementation approach—how to select style of approach.
- Definition of the plan—how to plan the implementation.
- Evaluation and improvement process—how to use feedback to make the process better.
- Special considerations—additional things to think about.

Although the techniques for assessment, strategic direction-setting, and Lean Management Systems are discussed here separately, many of them can be used across the other activities in an integrated manner, yielding tremendous results at the enterprise level.

Assessment Techniques

The fundamental purposes of the situation assessment process are to evaluate the total situation and to begin to hypothesize models of the situation. Figure 11.2 shows the suggested process with the assessment categories of desires and needs, culture, business situation, current initiatives, and goals and urgency wrapped up with a systemic assessment.

The totally up-to-date and completely comprehensive list of possible techniques that will address every situation is constantly expanding, since new and modified approaches are being developed almost daily. The following summaries have provided guidance to allow organizations to be very effective. ⚠ In fact, if an organization gets too comfortable with a rigid, specific template

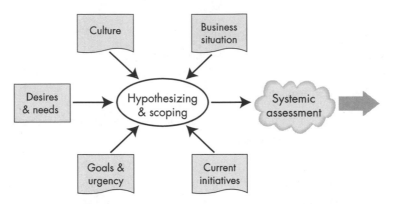

Figure 11.2: Situational Assessment Process Model

of techniques, there is a high risk that improvement over time will be limited. Therefore, each organization should constantly evaluate its level of success and constantly update its own table of techniques to optimize effectiveness.

The possible techniques for the macro assessment phase are almost endless. A short list of suggested techniques follows:

- Interviews
- Group sessions
- Questionnaires
- Site visits (observe operations)
- Process reviews (walk through the process)
- Process observations (witness actual work in process)
- Performance data reviews
  - Financial
  - Marketing
  - Operations
  - Customer programs
  - Product programs
- Review of existing plans

Individual lean implementation specialists may find it helpful to fill in the management system diagram chart (see Chapter 5) to visualize how the management system functions and to sketch out a business system map to visualize how the interactions operate.

The suggested areas to consider during this assessment process can be found in Figure 11.3.

Focus Area	Attributes to Consider/Evaluate
Desires and Needs	• Customers' desires • Organization's desires • Individuals' desires (Key managers and diagonal slice perspectives)
Goals and Urgency	• Driving forces • Gap to targets • "Problems" identified by management • "Problems" identified by diagonal slice interviews
Business Situation	• Clarity of direction • Leadership capability • Market forces • Level of waste
Current Initiatives	• What is currently going on? • Current processes • Current methods
Culture	• Level of empowerment • Anxiety level • Adaptive capability/flexibility • Organizational behavior • Level of process discipline
Organizational System	• Specific issues • System issues • System behavior • Adaptability • Commitment to improve

Figure 11.3: Key Assessment Considerations

Every situation is different; therefore, following a rigid, one-size-fits-all technique application sequence when doing an assessment will not necessarily yield a perfect answer in every situation. The intent should be to answer the following key assessment questions:

- What is happening now?
- What are the key pressures and issues?
- What is the organizational culture?
- What is the organizational system behavior?

Lean implementation specialists should use the techniques that will yield the best set of information and greatest insight in the allowable time frame. The thoughtful study of the assessment data provides a baseline understanding of the organization. To improve effectiveness, it is essential to consider these factors individually, as a group, and finally as an interaction when developing hypotheses for improvement and defining the appropriate techniques and approaches for the organization.

Strategic Direction-Setting Techniques

The strategic direction-setting process (i.e., defining strategic intent) was discussed in detail in Chapter 7 with several of its supporting techniques. Many possible methods or tools can be used at the detail level. The macro techniques that should definitely be on the options list include those shown in Figure 11.4.

Focus Area	Activity
Internal and External Environmental Analysis	• Concept Model analysis • SWOT analysis • Environmental assessment • Paradigm analysis • Values and philosophy analysis
Direction and Strategy	• Strategic planning • Market planning • Customer planning • Technology planning • Innovation planning • Product planning • Proactive development planning • Supply planning (including manufacturing) • Resource planning • Competence planning
Success Definition	• Metric and goal establishment • Initiative development • Action planning
Projected Results	• Financial planning
Implementation and Follow-up	• Policy deployment • Metric and goal management • Action and initiative management • Financial management

Figure 11.4: Techniques for Defining Strategic Intent

In a lean enterprise approach, the evaluation of the strategic direction ideally encompasses all elements and value streams within the organization under consideration. In a lean enterprise, all of the support activities to the major value stream work interactively in an efficient and effective manner to produce the maximum customer value and maximum business value in the minimum time at the minimum cost. In order for an organization to achieve these efficiencies, it must be aligned to meet a common strategic direction. The techniques of strategic direction-setting, when completed as described earlier at multiple levels in the organization, provide an excellent process for aligning the direction and thus making the content on which the organization needs to focus lean. Many of the techniques used in creating Lean Management Systems provide tremendous insight and guidance for improving the strategic direction of the organization.

IN THE REAL WORLD

In a recent client activity, the desire was to implement a lean strategic management process. The organization had just gone through a major restructuring and most of the organizational leaders were new to this particular business. A series of leadership planning sessions was scheduled to map the new direction, align the team, define the new management system, and define the implementation plan. In the very first strategic planning session, the group was introduced to lean concepts and value analysis (waste analysis). Also, a high-level flow analysis of the business relationships and structure was completed. This flow analysis map, coupled with the introduction to the concepts of lean, totally changed the group's understanding of the business process, and it helped them to determine the real strategic issues on which they should focus energy and effort. The concept model process and key issues discussion then yielded a much more enlightened dialogue.

Each of the ensuing sessions included an integration of strategic planning concepts and processes and lean management systems concepts and processes tailored to the specific top issues defined by the leadership group. This process enabled the new leadership team to redefine the entire management operating system in only a few months, launch their key initiatives with clearly defined targets, and remove approximately 30 percent of the daily work the managers had previously been attempting to accomplish unsuccessfully.

Key point: Using the concepts and techniques in creative combinations can provide tremendous leverage and progress.

Lean Management Systems Techniques

There are many possible techniques and supporting tools and methods for implementing Lean Management Systems. The highest order techniques have been shown in Figure 11.5 and categorized as key techniques, support techniques, and enablers (or enabling techniques).

Key Techniques
- Management system analysis
- Flow analysis
- Value analysis

Support Techniques
- Workplace organization
- Visual controls
- Consistent job practices
- Quick set-up
- Error proofing
- Project selection (opportunity targeting)
- Problem solving (root cause analysis)
- Planning methodologies

Enablers
- Communication
- Teamwork
- Consensus processes
- Empowerment/followership
- Lead-time reduction
- Systems thinking
- Lean organizational structure
- Metric management
- Change methodology
- Policy deployment
- Customer focus
- Involvement/engagement
- Leadership
- Coaching
- Training
- Statistical methods
- Risk management
- Alignment methodologies
- Meeting processes
- Action plan management

Figure 11.5: Lean Management Systems Techniques

Just as a skilled machinist needs to stock many tools to accomplish various machining jobs, organizations must learn to stock their toolboxes with the right tools for the work they will be called upon to accomplish. It is very likely that one technique will not meet every need completely. Therefore, it is the selection of the *set* of techniques that will best integrate with the organizational direction, culture, and specific needs that is the challenging task.

IN THE REAL WORLD

"We can only have one new process initiative, so what will it be?" was the question from the top executive. Many organizations have this type of exclusivity perspective about improvement techniques. An example of this and the confusion it can create is the situation many companies have experienced when trying to determine whether to implement lean or six sigma. Some describe lean as one approach, and six sigma as another, believing the two cannot be implemented simultaneously. Or they have a desire to categorize one as having higher importance than the other. This lean versus six sigma dilemma is based on the way they perceive processes and techniques interacting. Since they feel the need to have one controlling improvement philosophy (or program), they are delayed in getting started by endless debate over which philosophy is better and more encompassing, completely missing the point that each tool can be applied within either philosophy by targeting specific types of projects or by doing a common-sense integration of the techniques to meet the specific needs.

Key point: Organizations need to have numerous tools (techniques) in their toolboxes and they need to know how and when to use each tool. Different tools can be used as required in different parts of the organization—a disorganized shipping room may need workplace organization techniques, a laboratory doing many uniquely different tests may need quick set-up techniques, and an engineering development group may need flow analysis techniques with lead-time reduction concepts.

Systemic and Priority Considerations

From the assessment, one can begin to hypothesize potential solutions from the key issues and systems perspectives, as always, dealing with the most important issues first. Figure 11.6 shows a four-box matrix of priority-setting considerations with recommended action timing. In general, one should move from the lower left (i.e., an impact now with short-term action timing) to the upper right (i.e., a future impact with long-term action timing) in tying solution techniques to key issues, while exercising caution not to get trapped in the lower left box. It is important to properly balance across all four quadrants so that current and future issues are adequately addressed.

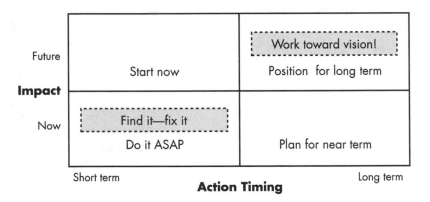

Figure 11.6: Technique Application Priority Matrix

In this hypothesis phase, lean implementation specialists should consider the system reaction to the possible techniques in a "Let's explore how that will work" mode. This means playing out the scenario to the end and considering potential risks, reactions, impacts, and consequences—and then defining improvements. Some questions to carefully consider in the systemic evaluation are:

- How have past improvement initiatives been accepted?
- What are the techniques that the organization and its management will likely support and implement?
- What improvements can be made to the technique or its implementation to increase its probability of success?
- How well will the organization accept these techniques and adhere to them?

• How committed is the leadership and the organization to really do what is required?

In many cases, the existing techniques being used by the organization have very valuable aspects and do not need to be replaced, but refined using lean concepts. The successful transition model usually includes leveraging some of the existing organizational techniques (or improved versions of them) and integrating them with the priority considerations. The less disruption created as the new techniques are implemented, the higher the likely organizational comfort and support. Therefore, as one begins to consider totally new

IN THE REAL WORLD

Always let the assessment define what needs to be done. In a recent client activity we were astounded that this particular organization had a culture of not listening. In addition, the organization made very few decisions and those that were made seemed to be undermined almost as soon as the decision meetings were complete. We concluded that this fundamental culture would not allow any strategic direction-setting or Lean Management Systems activity to flourish; therefore, the cultural problem had to be addressed. We took two actions. First, we instigated a communication and listening skills workshop and injected organizational development facilitators into the key meetings to provide quick, direct feedback. Second, we had a session on teamwork and decision-making, where the group defined how they would operate. We suggested a consensus definition (which we first heard from Mr. Willie Ozbirn, of Invensys, PLC) and they agreed. The consensus definition was: "Unless you are at least 80 percent certain that this idea or suggestion will not work, then you will support making it work." In addition, "Once an agreement is made, the group will stick together until the group has consensus to change the decision." This fundamental work enabled the next steps of setting direction and implementing Lean Management Systems to be very productive.

Key point: One must deal with the first issues first, and they may not always fit into the simple checklist. In many cases, the soft-side cultural issues must be addressed before the hard-side techniques can be effectively applied.

concepts, consideration should also be given to refinement of existing techniques, using the confirmed strategic direction and the new lean focus as a basis.

Before launching any new technique, it is necessary to integrate all of what has been uncovered and assess how the organization will deal with the technique and its implementation. After considering how the organizational system will behave, lean implementation specialists can adapt the implementation plan accordingly. Proper technique implementation can be challenging—like navigating an adaptive maze where the pathway constantly adapts to the last move and the entire maze changes over time.

Technique Selection Process

The technique selection and implementation process shown in Figure 11.7 begins once the organizational assessment from Figure 11.2 is complete. A possible list of techniques is then generated from the hypothesized analysis and the priority considerations. Then techniques can be selected, the style of implementation can be established, the implementation plan can be developed, and implementation can begin. Of course, performance feedback provides an input for continuous improvement of both techniques and implementation approaches.

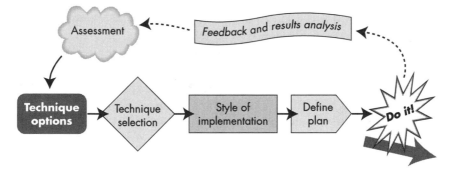

Figure 11.7: Technique Selection and Implementation Process

So which techniques should one select? This seems like a difficult question; however, the human brain is a wonderful processor of complex information. Over 70 percent of the time the best choices are clearly obvious by analyzing the issues and direction of the organization. The remaining 30 percent of the time requires more insightful analysis or expertise. Investing the time to understand the needs, and possible solutions to address those needs, is critical to selecting the techniques that will be most effective and that will build organizational momentum. The critical factor in technique selection is to drive an organized approach to *thinking* about which techniques will provide the best value in the specific situation being addressed.

One must be careful to avoid becoming so entangled in the myriad of possible improvement techniques that none are chosen to be implemented, or that the ones that have been started are not finished. The technique selection challenge is to select the best mix of techniques (i.e., tools, methods, approaches, or programs) from the endless supply of possibilities. A somewhat intuitive approach to targeting is the methodology typically used. It is fast, relatively easy, and usually yields fairly accurate results.

This intuitive approach is a facilitated discussion with a knowledgeable group covering the key elements of the organizational assessment, the performance needs, and the benefits of each potential technique. Some organizations prefer to call this approach the "expert panel" method, since the deciding group should be a panel of experts. When conducted properly, this discussion will yield excellent clarity around the techniques that will be most beneficial. A few additional crosschecks throughout the organization may be helpful to bring additional confirmation, when this is needed.

Figure 11.8 models the general thinking process for an intuitive approach. It includes a simple sorting process to determine which techniques fit by just rating them as "yes, they fit," "no, they do not fit," and "maybe they will fit (perhaps later)." The logic check step is to provide an avenue for discussion about the organizational system and its likely acceptance of the technique. Then the risk assessment discussion flows into the discussion of approach and timing. (An objective approach has been described in Appendix F.)

The real trick to optimizing results is to select a set of techniques and to integrate them so they make good business sense, given the specific situation at hand. Before making the final decision on which techniques to implement, the lean implementation specialist must consider the impact they will have on the organizational system and the likely organizational reactions, and the specialist must make certain that the benefits created offset the attendant risks.

Technique Implementation Approach

Careful consideration must also be given to the approach to be used (i.e., how to apply the techniques) and the level of intensity to be applied. The situation

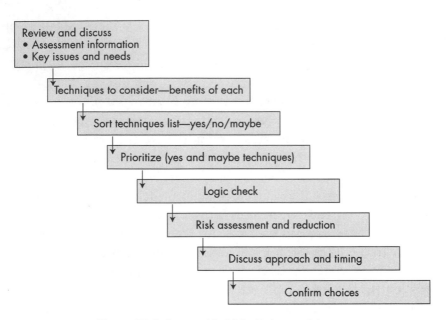

Figure 11.8: Intuitive Model for Technique Selection

assessments must be taken into account, paying particular attention to the leadership desires and support levels, urgency of the need to change, and existing initiatives and programs. There is a full range of possible approaches from "slow and soft" to "aggressive tyrannical," as shown in Figure 11.9. "Pressure" to be applied and "speed" for required results form the two axes of the diagram. These directly impact, or are impacted by, the coaching or learning style of the organization and the organizational disruption level desired. Defining five levels of approach along this continuum helps to further explain this concept. They are:

- *Slow and soft.* Low urgency, low pressure, slow speed of change is acceptable.
- *Integrated natural.* Integrate approaches with existing programs and allow change to occur at the natural speed of the organization.
- *Integrated pressurized.* Integrate approaches with existing programs and pressurize for quicker (i.e., time specified) change.
- *Fast do over.* Disrupt the organization by ending current initiatives and starting over with very high levels of pressure for fast change.
- *Aggressive tyrannical.* Total disruption to break old paradigms with extremely high levels of pressure (the bully approach).

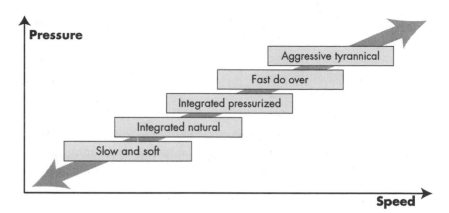

Figure 11.9: Continuum of Approaches

The two most generally successful approaches are aggressive tyrannical and integrated pressurized. Aggressive tyrannical works because it drives fast results and has no barriers. Integrated pressurized is successful because it leverages what has already been done and drives for fast results. Although the aggressive tyrannical approach is usually faster, it often has collateral damage and unintended consequences. However, it may be the only initial option in a crisis situation. Most organizations do not find they have the calendar time to proceed with slow and soft in today's dynamic marketplace.

Definition of the Plan

Defining the plan involves deciding what to do and how to do it, in detail. It should include the plan's requirements, approaches, and expected outcomes—much like a master plan. The general approach suggested is to:

- Select initial techniques.
- Apply and implement them with appropriate communication and training.
- Use what is learned throughout implementation to improve as the application is expanded.
- Add additional techniques when the organization is ready.

The key point of planning is to work through the implementation approach to reduce the errors and then to manage to the plan. A few additional hints that may be helpful are:

- Consider a learning-by-experiencing approach for training orientation—that is, employees learn to work by working.
- Consider the waves approach—that is, rolling out various tools over time so that the organization is not overloaded. If the group is mature, this timed rollout may be shared with the group as a part of the master plan. The speed of rollout can be varied to match the organization's capability and level of progress. In addition, this allows focus and acceleration of the concepts being implemented most successfully.
- Use care in communicating the plan. The message should be tailored to the specific stakeholder group, and it should be verified that it has been received as intended.

Evaluation and Improvement Process

Once implementation of the plan is progressing, it is necessary to analyze the effectiveness of the improvement activity and use the insight gained to improve the process. What approaches are working most successfully? Why? If the techniques selected do not work as well as desired or required, it is important to assess why and adapt them to correct the deficiencies, being certain to identify the cause of implementation problems. Which areas are struggling? Is it the technique, the application, or the organization that is limiting progress? Many organizations react to problems in implementation before it is clear whether the difficulties lie in the application of the technique, adequacy of the training, adequacy of support, cultural issues, or organizational issues. Effective problem-solving techniques and root cause analysis can help identify the true causes of implementation problems.

IN THE REAL WORLD

A client with whom we were working offered his views on the difference between a culture of real continuous improvement and the culture in his company. He said, "The improvement culture says 'Let's see *how well* it flies.' My company says, 'Let's see *if* it flies.'" He told us that this slight variation made a huge difference in the ability of his organization to make improvements. By working on this organizational paradigm and focusing on *"how well"* rather than *"if,"* we were able to help them adjust their attitudes to be more positive and view improvements as minor changes, rather than completely disruptive revisions.

In many cases, the adjustment of the technique based on initial imple-
⚠ mentation feedback is as important as the technique selection itself. As the
implementation approach is adapted, implementation specialists should
avoid thinking that because it did not work, we must do it over. It is reassur-
ing to the organization to communicate these adjustments as minor improvements based on organizational feedback. The same techniques will work
differently in different applications and organizational cultures, so adaptation
should be expected. In the end, it is developing a good solution for the specific situation at the right time that really matters.

For best results always:

- Analyze and improve as implementation proceeds.
- Watch for problems and address them quickly and appropriately.
- Evaluate lessons learned and apply the new understanding where
  appropriate in succeeding applications.

Special Considerations

Below are some additional ideas that have proven helpful in successfully
launching new techniques:

- Design an optimized solution for the specifics of the organization.
- Start with a pilot activity to test the concept and approach and then
  expand on a wider scale. One might start by selecting
  – A pilot area
  – A target product
  – A lead organization
- Leverage internal champions as change agents to coach and accelerate
  progress.
- Test with the management group and have them become the initial
  coaches.
- Use an internal team working with external consultants to add suffi-
  cient focus.
- Start with a limited number of new techniques in any one time period
  so that the organization is not overloaded.

Experience will improve the organization's ability to choose the right tool at
the right time, thus maximizing the value (benefit versus cost). Care should be
taken to ensure that the organization is reflecting on its learnings and dealing
with its paradigms in ways that will enhance the future implementation actions.

Techniques Selection Example Cases

The proper selection of the techniques to implement and the approach for implementation are crucial to the successful and expedient implementation of strategic intent and Lean Management Systems. Following are four simplified example cases, which are intended to demonstrate the analysis and thinking involved, based on four different situations.

Case 11.1

Two large multinational organizations were being merged.

Focus Area	Key Observations
Desires and Needs	• Integrate both organizations • Combine best practices of each organization without bias
Goals and Urgency	• Competitive pressures were tremendous • Merger was done with requirement to reduce redundancies
Current Initiatives	• Cost reduction • All other major initiatives terminated with merger activity
Culture	• Purchaser: high anxiety, inconsistent discipline • Purchased: high empowerment, good discipline
Business Situation	• Purchaser: just beginning waste reduction activity • Purchased: strong mid-level leadership, good market understanding and processes • Some customers concerned about merger
System Assessment	• Purchaser organization had a "we won" attitude • Purchased organization was not getting fair hearings
Improvement Implementation	

Techniques Selected	• Strategic organizational alignment:
	  – Teamwork
	  – Communication
	  – Strategic planning for all divisions, business units, and departments
	• Lean Management Systems:
	  – Management system diagramming to define a common cadence
	  – Process flow analysis—mapping teams for each major business process
	  – Best practices sharing

Approach Selected	• Integrated pressurized • High intensity focus on teamwork and balance from each organization

The merger allowed for a high-pressure focus and almost all managers really wanted to be involved to be able to influence the future direction and to promote their views. The joint approach to refining strategic direction and implementing lean techniques allowed for a smooth transition and freed up resources to address business opportunities that previously had been unsupported.

Case 11.2

A company operation was in financial trouble and had become uncompetitive.

Focus Area	Key Observations
Desires and Needs	• Rescue the company from bankruptcy spiral
Goals and Urgency	• Eliminate negative cash flow • Dire trouble—losing money at a rate that would shut the operation in seven months
Current Initiatives	• Draconian cost reduction/avoidance
Culture	• View any change as risky • "Living in the past" when things were good • Rely on top-down direction
Business Situation	• Company people did not realize they had serious competitive problems • Customers constantly complained that prices were too high and value was too low • Union was reluctant to accommodate change • Business skills were lacking throughout the organization
System Assessment	• Culture had never accepted fast change • About 50 percent of top management and 10 percent of employees seem to be concerned or desiring of change • Significant intergroup strife
Improvement Implementation	
Techniques Selected	• Strategic direction-setting by management staff • Quick assessment to define high priority targets • Lean Management Systems concepts—waste reduction • Initiatives management weekly • Lean manufacturing techniques
Approach Selected	• Aggressive • Focus on results, recognizing that people are going to be displaced

An aggressive approach was selected, due to the crisis of the situation. Management agreed that, after 12 months, if they survived, they would begin a culture rebuilding process. In addition, communication about what was happening and why it was necessary was a significant part of the overall process.

Case 11.3

A small business recognized a ten-year challenge and wanted to prepare in advance.

Focus Area	Key Observations
Desires and Needs	• Redirect company with a long term growth plan
Goals and Urgency	• Maintain employment (or grow) • Go slow so everyone can participate
Current Initiatives	• Suggestion program • QS9000 certification program underway • Exploring new markets
Culture	• Everyone is responsible for success • Everyone needs to be involved • Paternalistic concern for employees by owners
Business Situation	• Growth was slowing in traditional markets • Competitors were consolidating to become much larger • Profitable but declining
System Assessment	• Capable people • Business systems unusually good for company of its size • Strong fundamental management system
Improvement Implementation	

Techniques Selected	• Total involvement and engagement (involve everyone)
	• Strategic direction setting and strategic planning involving diagonal slice teams from top to bottom of company
	• Market analysis and planning
	• Lean Management Systems:
	  – Management system diagramming
	  – Process flow analysis—mapping teams for each major business process
	• Best practices sharing

Approach Selected	• Slow and soft • Focus on people and "family" culture

The slow and soft approach was selected because the challenge was viewed as being far in the future and the company history and family-like culture were extremely important to the owners and management team.

Case 11.4

A service company was at risk of losing its major customer due to lack of responsiveness (not meeting specific requirements).

Focus Area	Key Observations
Desires and Needs	• Keep business with current customers • Immediately improve relationship with major customer
Goals and Urgency	• Customer had given six months to improve by 50 percent
Current Initiatives	• Work harder—identify and punish the guilty
Culture	• Willing, relatively happy workforce • Somewhat internally focused • Customer satisfaction not given highest priority • Slowly moving from command and control to empowerment model
Business Situation	• Strategic plan assessment proved to be very good • Poor order entry and dispatch systems
System Assessment	• People seemed willing to try anything to fix the problem • People working hard but the processes seemed to breakdown • Significant expediting to make up for systems problems • Management team not yet ready to accept the customer's position
Improvement Implementation	

Techniques Selected	• Customer focus sessions for everyone with open discussion of current "score" every month
	• Lean concepts:
	  – Workplace organization
	  – Visual controls
	  – Process flow analysis—teams for each major business process (with extra focus on order entry and dispatch systems)
	• Communication to customer by managers and team members (status reports and listening sessions)

Approach Selected	• Fast do-over • Focus on people, customer, and speed in a systems thinking mode

This organization had to end some of its old practices toward people and move toward a more empowered model with a prime focus on improving the speed of response through waste reduction, flow enhancement, and increasing flexibility to deal with last-minute customer changes.

Summary

Selecting the right tool and technique set to accomplish the organization's strategic intent and achieve its potential may indeed be one of the most perplexing problems faced by the strategic leader. Sometimes it may feel like one is deciding where to place his or her bets at the roulette wheel. Use of the

IN THE REAL WORLD...

Several years ago we had the opportunity to work with a client in South Africa. We were retained to evaluate an operation within a large multi-national corporation, prescribe improvements, and assist the management in creating a plan to turn around the performance of the organization. Having never been to this country before, we did not know the people involved, their personalities, the situation, the culture, or how well this company was operating. We had three weeks to sort out everything and report recommended actions to top management. Given the situation this is a classic example of:

"Which tools should we apply to get the best results in the time available?"

We decided first to do an assessment of the organization by interviewing the management staff and many other people within the organization. Simultaneously, we started evaluating key metrics of performance by reviewing management reports. We also included a series of plant tours and interviews with people at all levels in the manufacturing operations to define the impact of the management approach in operations. We needed to better understand the culture of the country; therefore, we spent considerable time with various groups outside of work. We visited with people from various ethnic groups, at multiple societal levels, often in their homes. We visited schools, hospitals, and other businesses. We also met with the company's customers. By processing the external information and from the internal assessment activities, we were able to determine that the key problems facing the organization were: misalignment of the management staff with the managing director, a lack of focus on producing profitable results, a nonlean inventory system, and a manufacturing workforce desperate for improvement.

thinking process suggested will increase the likelihood of making a winning bet, and proper planning and implementation management increases the likelihood of successful, timely results.

The approach suggested requires rigorous analysis, systems thinking, and careful planning combined with experience and clear thinking. In review, the key steps are:

> We decided to implement a multipronged approach to address these issues. We chose to use strategic planning techniques to surface the issues of misalignment and lack of focus on profitable results. We also chose to implement initiative management system tools so that a detailed follow-up system would be in place. This provided a means to establish profit improvement initiatives, initiatives that lessened the causes of misalignment, and initiatives that would drive future implementation of lean manufacturing concepts. We recognized that, in order to improve the inventory system, general training on the subject of lean was required. Therefore, we initiated training classes for a large segment of the manufacturing organization, plus the management staff. The other intended benefit of this training was to create a forum to have dialogue about the problems in operations. The dialogue in the sessions was extremely productive. After training was completed, we helped design and initiate a lean inventory system, which also was critical to profit improvement.
>
> Many other tools could have been applied to the situation, but we chose the tools that would have the greatest impact in the limited time available. When you are working within your own organization, you are not limited to what can be accomplished within three weeks. Therefore, you can choose a broader set of tools and the appropriate sequence in which to apply them.
>
> We believe that we had a significant impact on the people in this organization. On our last afternoon at the factory location, as we were preparing to get in the car to go to the airport, we heard a commotion behind us in the parking lot. The people knew we were leaving, and they had spontaneously stopped working and assembled in the parking lot to thank us for teaching and helping them. This surprise was one of the most rewarding experiences that we have had in helping organizations.

- Assess the situation in detail.
- Consider the system implications.
- Sort through the technique alternatives and select appropriate techniques.
- Plan carefully.
- Launch and manage the implementation.

Select the set of techniques that best integrate to target resolution of the key organizational needs and to focus on improving the aspects required to achieve the organizational vision.

Technique selection and effective implementation will improve over time as the organization increases its improvement mindset, as new tools are experienced and developed, and as broad organizational implementation is achieved. One should expect that new techniques will require significant leadership support until they gain organizational confidence and become an ingrained part of the way things are done.

12

Making Things Better—
The Continuous
Improvement Mentality

*"You know you've achieved perfection in design, not when you have
nothing more to add, but when you have nothing more to take away."*

Antoine de Saint-Exupery—French Novelist and Aviator (1900–1944)

---

*Getting better and getting lean
are endless journeys.*

One can always get better. This fundamental philosophy of the lean continuous
improvement attitude is difficult for
many to truly internalize. It is critical for
long-term competitive success. Since most organizations require some time to
adapt to new ways of operating, and they are not able to move in giant steps,
the time and energy required should not be underestimated.

The organizational challenge is to
build a culture that *truly* embraces
this concept.

---

*The question: When will we be as
good as we possibly can be?
The answer: Never.
The good paradigm: We can
always get a little bit better.
It is, after all, an endless journey.*

Continuous Improvement
and Continuous Change

Successful, improving, adapting organizations have learned that chaos is not
likely to fix itself overnight. A long-term perspective with a short-term focus
on high-priority opportunities has been demonstrated to be the winning

approach, much like the old adage, "How does one eat an elephant?" The answer: "One bite at a time." Care must be taken to start "biting" at the right place, working through the improvement process. Figure 12.1 depicts this approach as a mountain, since many people describe their chaotic situation as being buried under a mountain of work and problems.

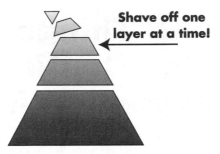

Shave off one layer at a time!

Figure 12.1: Focus on the Key Challenges and Opportunities

Improvement is the engine that drives progress.

Everyone wants to be on a winning team. Progress makes the team feel like it is winning, which motivates people to want to stay on the team and to keep winning. Everyone knows that progress requires change, yet so many organizations do not want to make change. The change paradox is that if we stay the same we cannot make progress, yet we do not want to change. Max De Pree (CEO of Herman Miller, Inc.) said it very well when he said, "We cannot become what we need to be by remaining what we are."[1]

It is so easy to say that we believe in continuous improvement, yet not really mean it—or understand what it truly entails, as is highlighted in the following Eli Goldratt quotation.

Any improvement requires change.
Any change results in a lessening of security.
People resist any lessening of security.
Therefore, people resist improvement.

Eli Goldratt—Author and Systems Improvement Expert

1. Max De Pree. *Leadership Is an Art*. New York: Bantam Doubleday Dell Publishing, 1989, p. 100.

Is the team really ready to change and progress? It will require:

- Desire to change
- Willingness to change
- Commitment
- Effort and perseverance
- Follow-up

The good news is that any positive effort will make the organization better.

Continuous Improvement

The art of improving the business management system requires balancing the complementary processes of analysis and systems thinking, as shown in Figure 12.2.

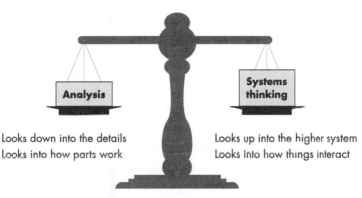

Figure 12.2: Balance Systems Thinking and Analysis

Analysis requires delving into the details of the steps that make up a management system, how they work, and what can be done to improve them. Systems thinking must be applied to develop understanding of how the particular management system fits into the overall business, and whether the improvements being considered will make the system more effective (or have detrimental side effects).

The management system of any organization operates in a dynamic environment. It must constantly deal with new situations and different people. This interaction causes constant mutation of the system. In virtually all organizations, there is both a formal and informal system of how work is done. Mutations are evident in the informal system. Often the informal system is an improvement over the formal system, but its very existence is a form of waste. As discussed in Chapter 5, constant vigilance is required to minimize the gap between the formal and informal systems and thereby optimize the leanness of the management system. The process of keeping the business management system lean and improving is never ending.

The following list provides a few hints on approaches that have been successful in driving continuous improvement and instilling it as a part of the long-term culture. Leaders of the organization should:

- Regularly ask, "How do we do work here, and how can we do it better?" Everyone in the organization should ask this question to gain ideas for improvement at all levels.
- Establish market-based goals. This is one of the best ways to guide an organization in trying to catch up to or stay ahead of the competition. The desire to catch up to where the competition is, or to our projection of where they will be, can be an extremely powerful motivation. Once the organization has caught up with or is ahead of the competition, then a more strategic methodology will be required to set appropriate goals to drive continuous improvement. A "We must keep improving by X percent per year because our competition is right behind us" approach can continue to drive progress.
- Hold periodic learning reviews (at least yearly). Then drive the lessons learned into the system. During these learning reviews make sure to resolve any specific issues, resolve any system weaknesses that allowed the issue to occur, and ensure that the lessons learned are spread across the entire organization. Be sure to celebrate the results of the event.
- Host a review with companies from other industries to share approaches, results, and learnings. Even preparing for this meeting will drive improvement. (Many organizations have experienced huge step-function changes in progress from this type of activity.)
- Establish a strategy and goal around time spent on improvement. Many organizations find that investing as little as one hour per week on improvement yields a tremendous performance improvement.

Change Methods

Continuous improvement requires change. The majority of change efforts in organizations do not succeed in achieving their desired outcomes. The failure rate is estimated at between 60 percent and 80 percent, depending on the measurement methodology. This fact should alarm everyone who is trying to make organizational change work. They should begin to ask why?

Why do organizational change efforts often fail? What made the successful efforts successful? The common characteristics of successful changes include:

- A clear reason to change (see Figure 12.3):
  - Justification for action and letting go of the old ways.
  - Reasons that are noble or personal are more empowering than "just to make more money for the company" or to win the boss a larger bonus.
- An urgent need to improve:
  - Reason to move quickly since most long-term actions wane before completion.
  - An imminent threat was recognized, so time could not be wasted and almost anything could be considered.
- A strong set of leaders:
  - Leaders with a consistent approach.
  - Leaders with a process for driving and supporting the change.
  - Leaders with a firmly held focus (no backing down).

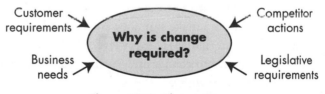

Figure 12.3: Change Drivers

Organizational change and organizational culture change is tremendously challenging. Many organizations that are at the edge of death will still not accept the need for change in their behavior. Others at the brink have been able to internalize the need to change and have stepped up to the challenge. The following list identifies some of the key lessons learned from successful change initiatives:

- Communicate, communicate, communicate.
- Make it real—that is, justify changes based on customers, competitors, and actual data.

- Focus on the plan, skills, rewards, resources, and actions.
- Demonstrate the new way.
- Treat everyone like they are important, part of the solution, and part of the team.
- Communicate the benefits of the change.
- Involve the group in making the plan (at every level).
- Build flexibility into improvements made.
- Develop multifunctional skills.
- Define the key approaches that will be used.
- Balance resources across the organization as changes are made.
- Reward teams rather than individuals.
- Encourage everyone to think—complete work tasks in ways to build business thinking.
- Give people ownership of the change.
- Set goals (targets) for all key requirements, but keep the list short enough to be measurable and meaningful.
- Set goals for increasing the rate of improvement and measure the rate of improvement.
- Form change-oriented teams to push the organization's abilities and keep the teams flexible.
- Reduce organizational churning (i.e., people movement) so everyone begins to own their business processes.
- Develop self-starters and make sure they are involved.
- Encourage the desired changes at every level.
- Communicate the need to change and the importance of achieving the goals at every opportunity.

Systems thinking combined with organizational cultural understanding can enlighten the change agents about key pressure points and roadblocks. Open-minded listening and the ability to use adaptive learning are great assets when attempting to make significant change in well-developed organizational culture systems.

Breaking Paradigms

A paradigm is a pattern, model, or example (per Webster's dictionary). Organizational paradigms are often manifested as a set belief or way of

IN THE REAL WORLD

"Blocking" paradigms can be extremely paralyzing when trying to improve organizations. It is critical when assessing an organization to consider which paradigms are real and which are imaginary. A few examples of imaginary ones we have experienced highlight the significance of assessment.

We were once trying to help a client company improve its product and market strategies, but the organization had always been told that they had a world-class product and were the lowest cost producer, so they believed nothing needed to be changed. In this case the paradigms were retold and spread as propaganda until almost everyone believed them. The reality was that they were one of the highest cost producers and they had a relatively uncompetitive product with no particular advantage. Until these paradigms were broken the organization continued to work on the wrong things and did not address the deficiencies.

In improving the management system for a large organization it was recognized that the majority of people were convinced that they were already doing everything right and as lean as possible. This organization had been successful in comparison to the rest of the corporation and was viewed as the example to follow. The people naturally assumed that they were successful and the role model because of their outstanding management prowess—therefore, they must be doing it right. Actually, their product line was in a different location on the life-cycle curve (i.e., it was still growing) than the rest of the corporation's product lines. The accolades they were receiving had nothing to do with their management system—it was just luck of the life-cycle calendar. This false paradigm, that they were outstanding managers, had to be dispelled before any significant progress could be made.

These types of paradigms are difficult to address. Many times the change agent will be accused of terrible offenses as the sensitive issues are addressed. However, left unchallenged, this type of paradigm will drive activity and actions toward the wrong conclusion.

Hints: Consider addressing ingrained, personally sensitive paradigms slowly and with significant supporting data. Also, consider preliminary one-on-one discussions before any group discussions are undertaken.

behaving that prevents the organization from exploring new ways of understanding or better ways of working. They can affect organizations in both positive and negative ways. Paradigms are helpful when they allow people to apply appropriate learnings to new situations. However, they can paralyze an organization when outdated doctrine is accepted as if it were the absolute truth.

A helpful paradigm example would be, "Top management will always listen when you have a solid business case justification." Harmful examples include, "Nobody makes any money in this business" or "Top management will never approve of any of our ideas."

Helpful paradigms often protect us from dangerous situations or from wasting effort on approaches that have been proven not to work. On the other hand, harmful paradigms can cause us to accept as truth those things that have not been proven. The tricky part is identifying which paradigms are helpful and which are harmful. Some may be both, for example: "Touching a hot stove can cause serious burns." This paradigm may lower the risk of getting burned, but it may also make some people afraid to touch any stove—even a cold one.

All organizations have paradigms. Thinking about paradigms is hard work and requires open-mindedness and a willingness to explore fundamental beliefs. Figure 12.4 shows a model for addressing paradigms in a direct, an indirect, or a combined methodology. If the culture of the organization is very open and trusting, the direct approach can be used. If the culture is not open or trusting, then the direct approach is likely to be unsuccessful. In this case

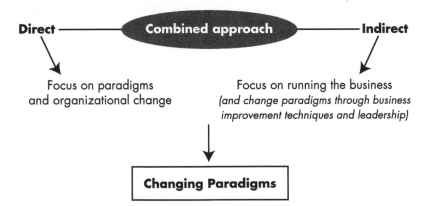

Figure 12.4: Process for Changing Paradigms

the organizational change agent may have to synthesize paradigms from group discussion or individual interviews and address them through indirect methods. Of course, the combined approach is optimal. Paradigms are a part of the organizational culture, so organizational systems thinking will be required to move the perspectives.

A quick culture assessment can be done individually on a small sample before attempting a large group endeavor. Leaders can ask each individual in a smaller group to describe the organizational culture in terms of:

- Openness
- Trust
- Integrity
- Teamwork
- People
- Other topics that seem pertinent

These concepts can then be processed with the organizational systems understanding to support a more fruitful group discussion of paradigms.

How does one find organizational paradigms? Listen for these common introductions to paradigms:

- Everybody knows...
- We tried that *once*...
- We are not ever going to do that again.
- It is impossible to...

Process worksheet headings for a group discussion of organizational paradigms are shown in Figure 12.5. The worksheet is designed to document the answers to the following questions:

- What are the key operating paradigms of this organization?
- Are they helpful or harmful?
- What are the requirements for these paradigms to be successful or true?
- Are these requirements sustainable?
- What is the impact of these paradigms?
- What actions are required?

The intent of documenting the organizational paradigms is to understand them, take immediate action to modify the key blocking ones, and to improve the management system processes to address any other restraining ones.

Paradigm	Help or Harm	Requirements	Sustainable	Impact	Actions

Figure 12.5: Group Paradigm Worksheet

IN THE REAL WORLD

While working with a client group composed of people from sales, marketing, engineering, finance, and manufacturing on a fundamental strategic planning and market strategy session, a discussion ensued as to whether a different market segment for an existing product should be pursued. One of the people from sales was within a year of retirement, and it was clear to all that his intent was to have smooth sailing for the next year. When this new unfamiliar market segment was discussed, our sales friend said, "Everyone knows it's a lot more expensive to do business in that segment than in the area where we have been very successful." As consultants who were unfamiliar with the market segment being discussed, we did not know whether it was more expensive or not to do business in this market segment. However, when we heard the catchwords "everyone knows" and knowing the personality of the individual making the statement, the words *"PARADIGM! PARADIGM! PARADIGM!"* appeared to be flashing before us in red lights. We told the group that this statement certainly sounded like a paradigm and engaged them in an exercise to determine the validity of the paradigm. By the time the analysis was complete, it was clear that it was no more expensive to do business in this market segment than in the ones with which our client was already familiar. By getting the group to challenge this paradigm, and to determine it to be false, our client was able to identify significant opportunities that otherwise would have been ignored. They were also able to identify a person in their sales organization who might need "special motivation."

Willingness to Challenge

The key to having a healthy continuous improvement mentality is to be willing to challenge accepted doctrine. Virtually everyone has experienced situations like the one depicted in the "Real World" story just told. It is management's job to create an environment where challenging the accepted norm is the expected behavior. However, challenging in a positive manner is a tightrope walk. There must be a balance between making certain that negative paradigms are not inhibiting positive actions, and that challenging all paradigms unnecessarily is not bringing progress to a halt. The secret to success is creating an environment of continuous improvement where people expect to be challenged without becoming defensive. At the same time, when searching for ways to do things better, one must constantly be certain that the challenging behavior is having a positive impact and creating the desired results.

Summary

Continuous improvement and lean strategic implementation needs to become the way of everyday life. Long-term competitive advantage and sustainability will only be achieved by constant improvement. Lean continuous improvement is not a temporary program; it is an endless journey.

PERSPECTIVES

In our view, continuous improvement includes both experiential learning modifications and situational tailoring to meet the exact needs of the organization. With our firm belief in true continuous improvement, we expect many of the models, processes, and techniques discussed in this book will be improved and modified to meet specific application needs. Therefore, we ask you to set your expectation on seeing an improved version of the models and processes in the future.

We also expect to continue to improve our understanding and our processes and techniques. We trust you will have the same expectation for yourself, and as you use these approaches, that you carefully adapt and improve them to fit your organization.

13

In the End
It Is Leadership

Thinking is required...
Every day, every hour, every minute...
Every time–all the time!

Some leaders are truly extraordinary people with a unique set of skills that sets them apart from the rest of the population. However, many leaders are just normal, ordinary people who have the position and responsibility of leadership. The importance of selecting the right leaders for the specific situation cannot be overemphasized. The right leadership is critical. Leaders who drive progress, leaders who support the organization in making progress, and leaders who do not slow down progress are all on the positive side of getting things done and achieving results. Whether the leader is extraordinary or ordinary, the responsibility is the same—to get things done.

The key leadership responsibilities are:

1. Define the direction.
2. Improve the system and process design.
3. Motivate people through empowerment, learning, etc.
4. Provide positive reinforcement and break barriers.
5. Follow up and ensure progress.
6. Drive continuous improvement.

NOTE

We have included two chapters in this book on the subject of leadership. We cannot overstate the importance of the role of leadership in successful organizations. In our many years of working with organizations on four continents, we have never observed a successful organization where strong positive leadership was absent. In the best organizations that we have observed, not only was there strong leadership at the top, but also throughout all levels of the organization. Leadership was carefully developed and nurtured. In addition, we have observed the opposite impact, where poor leadership caused significant challenges. Good leadership is not a panacea that will fix any problem, but without it, organizations are rarely successful.

Leadership

There are many definitions of leadership in the hundreds of books on the subject. However, in the arena of implementing strategic intent, leaders need:

- *Courage* to do the unpopular and unpleasant.
- *Strategic vision* to define an attractive future.
- *Persistence* to stick to the plan through difficult times.
- *Adaptability* to adjust the plan to changing dynamics.
- People *motivation skills* to build ownership and great followers.
- *Insight* about the business, the organization, and themselves.

The leadership model in Figure 13.1 was shown earlier in Chapter 2 but is important enough to repeat here. Great leadership is built on a deep foundation of highly varied skills, supported by broad competence, and capped by strong values. Great leaders focus a significant part of their energy on enhancing the assets under their stewardship and increasing the value of the legacy they have been entrusted to oversee. Establishing a clear strategic intent and enabling a Lean Management Systems approach are two methodologies that can offer tremendous benefits in these areas of responsibility.

The fundamental leadership philosophy espoused in this methodology is one of total employee involvement and engagement. Three of the key cornerstones of this philosophy are ownership, "followership," and empowerment. Followership is a term used to describe the position or guidance of the followers of the organization. Organizations require good followers with followership skills, just as they require good leaders with leadership skills.

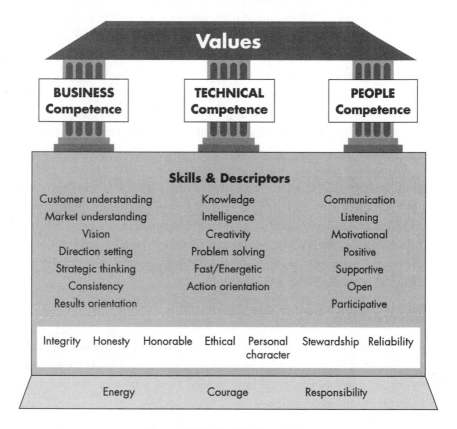

Figure 13.1: Model of Leadership

Ownership, followership, and empowerment are intertwined elements of good leadership that are worth an investment of managerial time and effort. This investment should include alignment discussions for the managers, clearly defining the philosophy in writing, communicating to the organization, coaching the organization, and continuous improvement. The return on this investment, when properly implemented, will be substantial. Each of these cornerstones is discussed in the following sections.

Ownership

Accountability, responsibility, and a feeling of personal ownership have been proven to be absolutely critical in driving results. When people who have ownership feel at personal risk, there is a higher probability that their performance will intensify and focus on enhancing their organization. Also, when people who are motivated by the feeling of ownership are allowed to participate and have real ownership, their performance certainly will intensify. Yet many large organizations seem to have a strategy to break personal ownership by constant rotation of the leaders. Smaller organizations have the advantage in this arena since everyone knows directly how their performance affects the results, and this drives levels of ownership that large firms should hope to emulate.

Ownership can be increased by continually reminding people to spend money as if it is their own and to make decisions as if the organization is their own. Tying compensation to performance results is also a proven effective method. In large organizations, an effective approach for increasing ownership is to create smaller units of responsibility and to staff them with teams of people who are held accountable for the performance of the unit. A note of caution for this approach is to be certain that these smaller subunits understand that the performance of the total organization must take priority over the optimal performance of the subunits.

Followership

Great organizations have outstanding followers at all levels. See Figure 13.2 for an assessment of the results with various combinations of leadership and followership. In other words, good leaders need good followers. But, of course, good leaders create good followers.

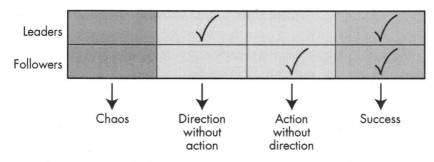

Figure 13.2: Leadership and "Followership" Are Both Required for Success

So what makes a good follower? First and foremost, a good follower must be willing to energetically implement the agreed management direction while accepting personal responsibility—assuming the management direction is ethical and legal. Good followers help others to be good followers by building alignment and organizational morale. A good follower should be willing to provide input to help shape the direction in which the organization will go. Input can be based on new ideas, concepts of better ways to complete a task, or new learnings that can be added to the overall knowledge base of the organization. Good followers should also be willing to provide feedback to their leaders. A good follower has the courage to help the leaders of the organization when they are moving in a questionable direction. Good followers also actively reinforce their leaders. Great followers have the wisdom to know how to approach leaders with appropriate feedback and inputs for improvement.

In the end, perhaps the most important role that a good follower can play is to be involved in the crucial activity of implementation—that is, getting things done. Once the direction is set, great followers implement. They continue to think about and to improve the details; however, they stay the course of the general direction. Great direction without implementation action will not yield success. Great generals without great armies do not accomplish very much. Great followers are an absolute requirement for getting things done and great leaders develop, nurture, and empower great followers.

Empowerment

No discussion of leadership is complete without touching on the issue of empowerment. For leadership to be effective there must be followership. For followers to be effective, leaders must empower people throughout the organization to take responsibility. Few organizations are successful if nothing is done unless the leader gives a specific command. Empowering people throughout the organization to take responsibility and to take action as required is a critical component of success. Leading and empowering is a balancing act. Empowerment does not mean the abdication of leadership responsibility. When leaders empower others to take action, they must carefully balance making people responsible for their actions with allowing them to fail and therefore learn (especially when the leader knows how to avoid failure). Obviously, empowerment will not be successful if the leader continually undermines or second guesses those who have been empowered. However, not allowing people who have been empowered to take appropriate action (particularly when the consequences are high) is equally unacceptable. Simply stated, good leaders know when to allow those who they have empowered to make mistakes and when to step in and prevent those mistakes.

Empowerment is truly about enabling people to be responsible, to have an ownership mentality, and to share in the stewardship of the business or organization. Effective empowerment requires that the key leadership aspects of Figure 13.1 (page 189) are solidly in place, and that appropriate follower-ship is understood by the organization. Empowerment is a delicate leadership balancing act. Not enough empowerment and one gets blind obedience, too much empowerment and one gets mutinous chaos, but just the right amount of empowerment yields fantastic results and organizational motivation.

Why Organizations Sometimes Fail to Get Things Done

Organizations sometime fail to reach their desired outcomes. The causes typically fit into one or more of the following, particularly where change is required:

- Lack of commitment.
- Not having a clear reason to change or make progress.
- Not following a systematic approach.
- Lack of discipline and follow-up.
- Trying to do too much, too fast.
- Lack of integration with existing strategies and systems.
- Trying to make the change without change agents.
- Lack of management consistency.
- Not including key stakeholders in the planning process.
- Not making the new way the only way for doing work.
- Lack of desire or willingness to change.
- Implementing a one size fits all solution, rather than creating specific solutions for the organization's unique requirements.
- Lack of courage among the leaders to make the change.

Implementation Agents Are Required

Organizations typically are not successful in implementing leadership and management systems improvement without strong implementation agents and top management commitment. The implementation agents must be:

- Expert in understanding people and in communication.
- Knowledgeable in lean concepts and processes.
- Able to help organizations to be honest with themselves.
- Able to diplomatically force issues to be resolved.
- Capable of creating winning approaches.
- Expert in applying the right approach at the right time.

The best implementation agents are:

- Without political or career attachments, so that difficult issues can be addressed.
- Experienced experts with a broad view of proven solutions.
- Competent in team alignment processes.
- Adept in solving difficult problems.
- Excellent in listening and converting what they hear into appropriate actions.
- Knowledgeable in a broad range of business processes.
- Coaches in their attitude and approach.
- Respected for their knowledge and ability.

When organizations are fortunate enough to have implementation agents with these skills, they should use them wisely and often. When they do not, they should seek external agents to improve the likelihood of success in driving successful change in less time.

IN THE REAL WORLD

Many organizations delay getting started. It is always a challenge to begin. A successful entrepreneur said he did not have the time or money to invest in improving his situation. When he was asked how much time and money the problems were costing him currently, he had to think for a long time. His answer finally became clear: "More than it would cost in time and money to improve it." To paraphrase; "I am paying anyway, I am just not writing a check." Recognition of the positive benefit to cost trade-off and ensuring that the potential causes of failure were understood and addressed allowed this businessman to reap significant rewards.

Summary

It would be great if the success of organizations did not depend so much on a small number of leaders. However, it appears that leadership is a key catalyst in defining success for most organizations. Leaders of teams, group leaders, department leaders, informal leaders, top managers, and CEOs can indeed make progress using the concepts of strategic direction-setting, lean, and getting things done implementation.

In the beginning it is leadership.
In the end it is leadership.
In the middle it is leadership.
Leadership is critical!

14

The Hope for a Better Tomorrow

Getting things done is based on practical, clear thinking:
- *Start at the end.*
- *Keep it simple.*
- *Think it through to the end.*

Defining the strategic intent of the organization can be done in a manner that aligns the entire organization:

- Decide what to do.
- Provide targets (metrics).
- Ensure that values are understood.
- Listen to the people in the organization.
- Provide strong positive leadership throughout the organization.

Lean implementation structure and discipline are critical to success:

- Keep the management system organized and focused (lean).
- Utilize lean concepts and techniques to remove waste.
- Provide structure and clarity.
- Provide methods (processes) to accomplish the goals.

Always continue to move toward the perfect state of the lean enterprise:

- Implement lean thinking and lean techniques into every activity.
- Focus the entire organization on the customer, value, flow, speed, and flexibility.
- Always work to get better.

Intellectual resource management is one of the key success factors for today's and tomorrow's organizations. All of the approaches that have been discussed include a component of people involvement. This involvement improves the analysis, improves the plan, improves the implementation support, and trains future organizational leaders.

The integrated approach to strategic Lean Management Systems—team building, strategic planning, lean management concepts, organizational re-engineering, systems thinking, and people involvement allows organizations to accomplish what may seem to be impossible. It uses proven methods to improve the focus and reduce the waste of valuable intellectual resources throughout the entire enterprise and to gain results in all aspects of a business or organization. It is truly all about getting things done.

Developing a fundamental management system that gets things done, that is lean, that allows for easy progress-tracking and redirecting, and that focuses the entire organization on adding value, can be accomplished. With patience, perseverance, and commitment, there will be tremendous improvement in the leanness and the effectiveness of the organization, and the organization will move toward the perfect state of the lean enterprise.

Those organizations that have clearly defined their strategic intent and implemented Lean Management Systems find their results to be:

- Increased ability to respond to opportunities.
- Enhanced customer satisfaction.
- Easier management task—that is, it becomes easier to complete the work of management.
- Enhanced employee satisfaction.
- Increased throughput.
- Greater return on assets.
- Improved competitiveness—that is, the organization is faster and more adaptable.
- Higher profits.
- Improved work atmosphere—a better place to work.

Tremendous opportunities are created when the waste is removed from an organization. It has also been proven repeatedly that people want to be on a winning team that knows what it is trying to do and how it will do it. In lean organizations people have more time to further improve, more opportunities are captured, motivation is high, and performance soars.

If your organization is not on this journey, it needs to get started now. The endless path of improvement has room for everyone, because no organization is ever quite as good as it could possibly be—there is *always* room for improvement. It seems that the best organizations are those that are working the hardest to improve. Getting things done is critical to making progress toward a better tomorrow.

The organizations that are willing to set a clear direction; support solid implementation; commit to improve; involve and train people; focus on customers, value, flow, flexibility, and speed; invest their energy; build a hatred for waste; strive endlessly for perfection; and reward the desired behaviors, will certainly reap the rewards of success!

Final Note from the Authors

We hope that more leaders will embrace these techniques to improve the competitiveness of their organizations for the benefit of the employees, the stockholders, and future generations. We strongly believe that this will separate the winners from the losers. We hope that your quest to improve will make you one of the winners.

Appendices

Contents

Appendix	Reference Chapter	Topic
A (page 201)	5	Lean Management Systems Hints and Worksheets
B (page 213)	7	Strategic Direction-Setting Worksheets
C (page 221)	8	Metrics
D (page 227)	9	Flow Analysis
E (page 235)	10	Implementation Formats
F (page 237)	11	Technique Selection: An Objective Approach
G (page 243)	12	Paradigm Discussion Processes

NOTE

These appendices are intended to provide additional process hints and formats that the practitioner may find helpful in the application of lean management systems and strategic intent implementation.

Lean Management Systems Hints and Worksheets

Lean Management Systems Hints List

Purpose

This lean hints list should be used as a reference to ensure that basic lean concepts have been considered. It is a basic set of "thought starter" points. Many of the hints may apply in several of the categories. Additional details, specific guidelines, and focus areas should be developed for individual situations when appropriate.

Customer Focus

- Make the system capable of providing what the customer wants when it is wanted (exactly what they want exactly when they want it).
- Design and control the system to meet all customer requirements and specifications.
- Focus program management on meeting customer requirements while achieving business goals.
- Review customer status and issues at the beginning of management meetings (when on the agenda) to demonstrate their priority.
- Evaluate customer satisfaction frequently and take corrective actions.
- Drive designs to meet customer needs at target costs.
- Drive proactive product development from market and technology needs.

- Establish customer teams (in any organizational structure) to build a focus toward the customer (this is particularly applicable in business-to-business situations).
- Consider frequent customer status progress reviews with top management.
- Organize work groups to optimize the flow of value to the customer.
- Work to understand actual customer needs from the customer point of view—do not treat all customers needs as the same and do not rely solely on past experience.
- Consider full- or part-time resident resources at your customer locations to speed responsiveness (business-to-business applications).
- Consider using a standard customer requirements definition process (e.g., house of quality).
- Establish a customer requirements review process (similar to a critical product design review).

Metrics: Measurements and Targets

- Understand key metrics and the impact of any improvement.
- Document before and after metrics of activities (visually is best).
- Consider metrics carefully—balancing results measures, process measures, and people measures.
- Make metrics and performance visible to the organization.
- Use the established metrics as part of the review and assessment process, not as after-the-fact scoreboard tallies.
- Require that all improvement projects define the expected metric improvement in the project business case justification.
- Keep the number of measures low for the bulk of the organization—understand the critical metrics versus the guidance and support metrics (which aid in diagnosing any performance issues).

Waste Reduction and Value Improvement

- Remember to reduce, combine, and eliminate all wasteful activity.
- Combine or eliminate redundant activities.
- Improve the methods used to complete value-adding activity.
- Define the communication system so that everyone understands what and how to communicate pertinent information.
- Establish checklists and forms for repetitive activities.

- Establish focused, scheduled review processes to drive issue resolution.
- Minimize required wasteful walking by considering facility size and floor-plan organization.
- Eliminate multiple handling of documents and materials.
- Reduce "For Your Information" (FYI) copies (paper and electronic).
- Support bottleneck activities to obtain maximum necessary throughput.
- Conceptualize designs with a lean manufacturing mentality.
- Assess all projects for lean content and design prior to investment (using checklists and a rating system).
- Eliminate or reduce multiple signature approval levels.
- Work on top causes of problems (i.e., root causes of highest priority issues).
- Understand the physical effects of problems versus their systemic causes and work to eliminate root causes of systemic problems across the organization.
- Do not create bureaucracy to control the system—make the work the easiest way to accomplish the desired result.
- Consider investment utilization on high-cost assets—should they be used two or three shifts per day?
- Consider which activities should be moved to worldwide low-cost areas to maximize benefits versus cost.

Flow Improvement

- Analyze the flow of people, materials, and information in each process.
- Analyze the flow of the process steps and key data of every process, with the challenge being to identify and remove as much waste as possible.
- Work to eliminate waiting, for any cause.
- Remove task interferences from the primary process path (i.e., the critical path).
- Locate receiving points close to point of use.
- Consider office layout to maximize flow and minimize waste.
- Design the system so the easiest way to do a task is the way it should be done.
- Eliminate physical barriers that impede flow and communication in the work area.

- Consider communication and value creation when designing office work areas (i.e., the need for privacy walls versus openness for communication).
- When private areas are required consider glass walls for visible openness.
- Use kanban systems to visually control critical processes.
- Limit available space for unnecessary inventory to accumulate.
- Develop business practices that support the needs of the next step in the value chain.
- Consider distributed rather than functional groupings—even in functional organizations.
- Do not develop large databases that require perfectly reliable information, complicated programming, or extensive data management—unless absolutely required and justified.
- Consider distributed, flexible computing systems rather than centralized ones—using centralized systems only where wide access is necessary.

Speed and Flexibility Enhancement

- Establish a simultaneous development approach.
- Co-locate simultaneous development teams consisting of applications, product design, manufacturing design, and others. Teams can be organized by customer, product, system, etc., but should be small in size.
- Use cross-functional teams wherever beneficial.
- Develop multifunctional workers who can easily support their team needs.
- Establish a flexible workforce to adapt to changing market requirements.
- Implement risk management processes to reduce surprises and to deal with issues earlier.
- Staff flexibly and appropriately for the work to be done.
- Manage and develop resource competency.
- Consider cradle-to-grave responsibility on key projects.
- Make development teams responsible for production launch effectiveness (avoid the throw-it-over-the-wall syndrome).
- Reduce people and organizational churning to build competence (maintain a stable core resource base).

- Critically evaluate the time required to complete tasks and improve through waste reduction.
- Consider outsourcing nonstrategic activities.
- Consider outsourcing activities where the organization is not competitive and does not intend to become competitive.
- Set targets for the time required to complete tasks and manage to those targets with frequent improvement required.
- Focus on critical path activities and do not bog down work processes by grouping with noncritical details.

Quality Improvement

- Reduce the number of work methods to reduce variation of process activities.
- Choose the best method and use it consistently.
- Provide visual aids to remind workers of quality risks and preventive actions.
- Make quality everyone's responsibility by working to reduce the quality "department" size to one—the quality manager (the position is required by many quality system certifications).
- Choose the most effective tool that achieves optimum cycle time, meets quality requirements, meets safety standards, and is easy to use.
- Ensure that critical machines and equipment have high uptime.
- Use preventive maintenance processes to maintain high uptime.
- Have redundant capability on critical processes until uptime is achieved.
- Use error-proofing techniques to prevent or detect errors.
- Focus first on process capability, then error-proofing, and, finally, detection as a last resort.
- Integrate error-proofing activities with consistent job practices (i.e., standardized work).
- Use FMEA (failure mode and effects analysis) and risk priority assessment to define error-proofing requirements and priorities.
- Consider the physical body dimensions of all team members when designing or modifying workplaces—design in flexibility when possible.
- Spread countermeasure activity throughout all similar processes and evaluate potential of the root cause to create problems in nonsimilar areas.

Business Management

- Make all plans *lean*—keep a clear focus (usually less is more).
- Communicate business strategy to direct the organization.
- Document and communicate strategic, market, customer, technology, product, and manufacturing plans.
- Make plans visible.
- Develop clear objectives, goals, and action plans.
- Establish a rigorous action plan follow-up system.
- Communicate management control system requirements and test for understanding.
- Communicate financial status and performance to goals frequently.
- Push decisions and authority to lowest possible levels.
- Continue on the endless path to empower the organization.
- Train the organization on positive leadership techniques.
- Clarify responsibilities while avoiding the tendency to overdefine.
- Use life cycle and unit costs to drive decision-making (combined with return on net assets).
- Develop more capable suppliers so they can be relied upon more heavily.
- Maximize communication effectiveness through focused communication procedures and channels.
- Use competitive analysis and benchmarking techniques to drive action.
- Understand resource balance (% customer support, % development, % R&D, % administrative, etc.) so that time can be invested on the right things.
- Analyze exceptions to lean concepts and ensure they are business-case justified.
- Make sure employees feel they are responsible for the business, have control of the activities they are performing, and that they can make a difference by effectively doing their jobs.
- Challenge the organization to beat the competition and continually improve.
- Avoid forcing additional approval steps to gain control of nonlean processes. Work to address the nonlean issues and causes.
- Make as few policies as possible—and only those that will be fully implemented and supported.
- Make active continuous improvement a key part of the business system.

Business System Matrix

Figure A.1 is intended for processing group perspectives on waste in organizations, processes, or departments. Its application is discussed in Chapter 5.

	Process 1	Process 2	Process 3	Process 4	Process 5	Staff	Other
Employees**							
Budget **							
% Customer Value Add							
% Business Value Add							
% Waste							
Opportunity $							
Probability of Success							
Target $ Improvement							

** = Dedicated to this activity   Note: Process may be replaced by department

Figure A.1: Business System Evaluation Matrix (or Macrowaste Evaluation Worksheet)

The discussion on the business system evaluation matrix should link to the nine types of waste. In addition, adding rows to the table that include any of the following questions that apply can also add a further depth of discussion to the analysis and stimulate thinking on how well the processes are actually working.

- How much of the activity is crisis mode or late?
- How much of the work is done outside of the standard process?
- How much time is spent waiting on approvals, specifications, etc.?
- How much time is spent in intergroup communication?
- How much correction, or redoing, is required?
- How much special expediting is required?

Management Systems Diagram Worksheet and Format

A description of the management system diagramming process can be found in Chapter 5. The worksheet in Figure A.2 outlines the key questions to be addressed and may be helpful in the application of the process. Figure A.3 provides a blank format for the management system diagram. Remember, the management system diagramming process can be applied at any level of an organization and multilevel diagramming can be enlightening in the search for improvement opportunity.

Management System Diagram Element Worksheet

Management Responsibilities
- What are our management team responsibilities?
- Are there some required and some desired responsibilities?

Major Tasks Schedule
- What are our major required activities throughout the year?
- What are the key milestones (business plan, budget, etc.)?

Schedule of Reviews
- What reviews (approvals, critical evaluations, or information sharing discussions) need to be held to deliver our responsibilities?
- Which reviews require our participation to ensure we meet our obligations?
- How often are these reviews needed?

Standard Meeting Schedule
- What meetings are required?
- What events drive the requirement for meetings?
- Which meetings are we expected to attend?
- What meetings do we need to call?
- Which meetings are called as needed and which are regularly scheduled?
- How do we make these meetings meaningful, effective, and efficient?

Control Processes
- How will we ensure that our good intentions are fulfilled?
- See "Control Processes" in Chapter 5 (page 65).

Communication
- How will we communicate to the organization?
- See "Communication" in Chapter 5 (page 66).

Organizational Linkages
- What linkage and coordination with other parts of the organization need to be accomplished?
- What do we need to share, and with whom, across the organization?
- When is linkage communication required (prior—to gather inputs, or afterwards—to communicate results)?

Figure A.2: Management System Diagram Worksheet

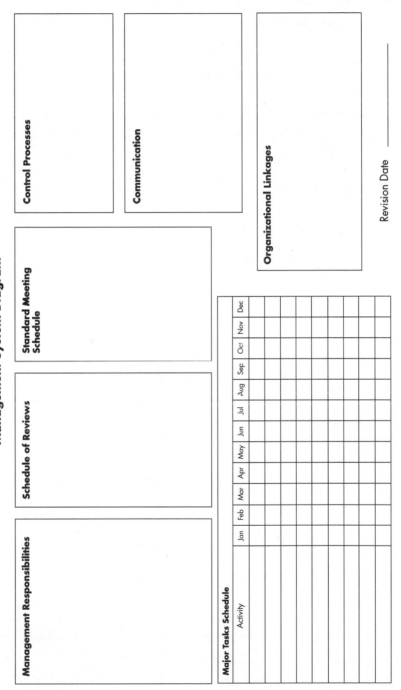

Figure A.3: Management System Diagram Format

Waste and Workplace Organization—
Observation Surveys

Instructions

- Apply the surveys in Figures A.4 and A.5 after some orientation on value add and waste.
- Have the group do a walk-through of the selected focus area and document the waste and workplace organization aspects on the survey forms.
- Discuss as a group.
- Develop an improvement plan.

Waste Survey Sheet

Department or Area: _____

Waste Observed Write the specific waste observed in the space below and then mark the column for the type of waste. Attach additional sheets if required.	Overproduction	Correction	Processing	Motion	Waiting	Conveyance	Inventory	Creativity	Motivation

Date: _____   **Observer:** _____

Figure A.4

Workplace Organization
Observations Data Sheet

Department: _____ Date: _____

Location: _____ Observer: _____

Criteria	Observations
Sort	
Is there unnecessary equipment/devices?	
Are there unnecessary personal items?	
Are there unnecessary tools or process equipment?	
Is there unnecessary inventory (supplies, storage, WIP)?	
Set in order	
Is everything in its place?	
Are items properly stored?	
Are visual controls used?	
Are items/locations labeled?	
Are things placed so they are easy to see/use?	
Shine	
Are the work areas clean? Desks? Floors? Data storage areas?	
Are cleaning materials available and stored properly?	
Are safety requirements met? Safety glasses, shoes, hearing protection?	
Standardize	
Is the work performed in the same way every time?	
Are operator instructions in place and being followed?	
Are quality standards visible and being used?	
Sustain	
Are there regular housekeeping checks?	
Do information boards have up-to-date information?	
Are responsibilities clear? Are they posted and up to date?	

Figure A.5

Strategic Direction-Setting Worksheets

The following strategic planning process concepts are provided as simplified starting guidelines to create a basis for understanding. They should be used in conjunction with the processes discussed in Chapter 7. One may choose to modify or improve them for specific cases. Users should feel free to combine these approaches with other traditional methods and organizational experience.

Strategic Business Plan Outline

- Vision
- Mission
- Philosophy and Values (optional)
- Objectives (3 to 5—more if required)
    - 1
    - 2
    - 3
    - 4
- Goals (1 to 5 for each objective—more if required)
    - 1.1 to 1.5
    - 2.1 to 2.5
    - 3.1 to 3.5
    - 4.1 to 4.5

- Strategies (3 to 5—more if required)
  - 1
  - 2
  - 3
  - 4
- Action Plans/Initiatives
  - 1 to 100 (20–50 initiatives is a typical number)

Concept Model

The concept model format in Figure B.1 should be used in conjunction with the process discussion points from Chapter 7.

Concept Model for _____

Customers	Customer needs	Key buying factors	Key success factors	Company needs	Products

Competitors	Strengths	Weaknesses	Opportunities	Threats

Figure B.1: Concept Model Format

The key market and business questions shown in Figure B.2 may be helpful in building a more complete understanding of the situation surrounding the market, customers, competitors, and technology. This understanding may be helpful in building a more robust concept model.

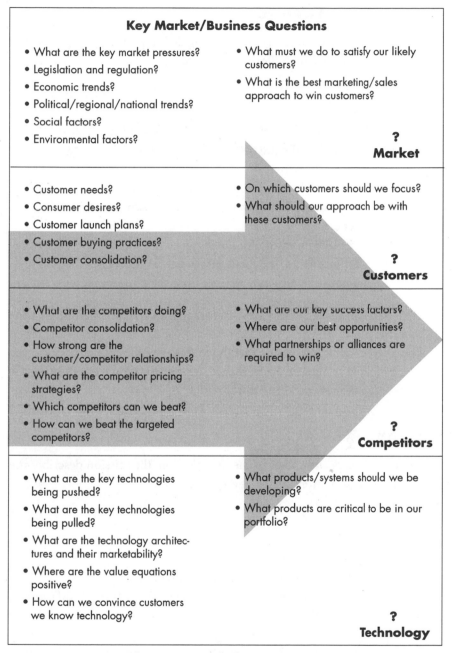

Key Market/Business Questions

- What are the key market pressures?
- Legislation and regulation?
- Economic trends?
- Political/regional/national trends?
- Social factors?
- Environmental factors?

- What must we do to satisfy our likely customers?
- What is the best marketing/sales approach to win customers?

? Market

- Customer needs?
- Consumer desires?
- Customer launch plans?
- Customer buying practices?
- Customer consolidation?

- On which customers should we focus?
- What should our approach be with these customers?

? Customers

- What are the competitors doing?
- Competitor consolidation?
- How strong are the customer/competitor relationships?
- What are the competitor pricing strategies?
- Which competitors can we beat?
- How can we beat the targeted competitors?

- What are our key success factors?
- Where are our best opportunities?
- What partnerships or alliances are required to win?

? Competitors

- What are the key technologies being pushed?
- What are the key technologies being pulled?
- What are the technology architectures and their marketability?
- Where are the value equations positive?
- How can we convince customers we know technology?

- What products/systems should we be developing?
- What products are critical to be in our portfolio?

? Technology

What strategy set will allow us to WIN?

Figure B.2: Key Market and Business Questions

Key Success Factors

Key success factors are extremely important in defining strategy as is discussed in Chapter 7. They have the following characteristics:

- Key success factors are attributes or capabilities that differentiate winners from losers.
- It is unlikely that there are more than a few key success factors:
  - The more specific the better.
  - The fewer the better.
  - Discriminate *key* from *important* factors.
- Key success factors change over time as the environment, industry, and market change:
  - Continually monitor and assess.
- Key success factors are the focus for successful strategy development.
  - Different strategies may emerge from the same key success factor.

The development of key success factors should be given significant time and consideration. The best strategies are developed from a very short list of insightful observations from the integrated understanding of customers, the market, potential competitive advantages, the organizational capabilities, the organizational desires, and the future trends.

Mission

Based on the beliefs and values of the organization, the mission describes the fundamental reason for existence. It answers:

- Who do you serve?
- What do you offer?
- How do you serve?

It provides the basis for what you are and do today.

The mission statement should also answer these three fundamental questions:

- Who?
- What?
- How?

Distilling the mission statement into a crisp, meaningful, and short set of words requires creative writing.

Vision

In creating the vision for an organization, it is usually very helpful to define the current state vision, and ideal (perfect) state, and then to process a desired state. These are typically lists of attributes to describe the situation in each of the three states (current, ideal, and desired). It is highly recommended to complete the mission statement before working on the vision, as this helps to set a reference point for discussion.

The vision statement answers the questions:

- Who?
- What?
- How?
- Where?
- When?

Distilling vision statements requires creativity and writing skill.

Typical Business Objective Categories

The typical categories for objectives in business organizations include:

- Customer
- Product/service—value/competitive advantage
- Operations
- Financial
- Market position or growth
- Quality (for some organizations)

Strategy Development

The following three approaches for strategy development have been successfully used to help groups distill their thoughts into a succinct strategy set. Successful strategy is developed from a limited few key success factors. The processes discussed help to analyze, and better integrate, what organizations are doing and what they should be doing. In addition, a quick process for evaluation of competitor strategy is shown as a building-block analysis.

Design-Build-Sell Strategy Process

The design, build, and sell strategy set (also called specify, procure, and sell for service and sourcing organizations) focuses the strategy team on three areas and then considers current strategy, the ideal strategy, and the desired strategy as shown in Figure B.3.

Area	Current Strategy	Ideal Strategy	Desired Strategy
Design or Specify			
Build or Procure			
Sell			

Figure B.3: Design-Build-Sell Strategy Process

The Business Functional Strategy Process

This process categorizes the typical functions in a business and analyzes the strategy like the design, build, and sell approach by considering current strategy, ideal strategy, and desired strategy. The typical categories include:

- Market (or Marketing)
- Sales
- Advertising
- Technology
- Finance
- Operations
- Supply
- PC&L (Production Control and Logistics)
- Distribution
- HRM (Human Resource Management)
- Purchasing
- Product or Service

Competitor Reaction Strategy Process

Many times it is helpful to consider the impact of a proposed strategy set on the market and on the competitors. The process chart shown in Figure B.4 can help the thinking in this area, especially in a group setting.

Your proposed strategy?	What the competition might do?	What you believe the competition will do?	What would be your usual reaction?	What your reaction must be?	What proactive action can be taken?

Figure B.4: Competitor Reaction Strategy Process

Competitor Strategy Comparison

Most organizations know a significant amount about their competitor's strategies and the discussion and documentation chart of Figure B.5 helps them to gather and distill this knowledge and provide insight into how to better predict and deal with likely competitor actions and reactions.

Strategy/ Category	Competitor 1	Competitor 2	Competitor 3	Competitor 4
Price				
Promotion				
Product				
Technology				
Support				
Supply				
Alliances				
Customer Relationships				

Note: Product can include services. Support can include before and after sales service. Supply can include wholly owned operations and suppliers.

Figure B.5: Competitor Strategy Comparison

Typical Business Strategy Categories

The typical categories of strategies in organizational business plans include:

- Customer approach
- Growth
- Product/Service/Technology
- Market approach
- Supply
- Operations
- People/Teams/Management
- Quality (for some organizations)
- Civic and environmental responsibility (for some organizations)
- Continuous improvement

Of course, many others may be applicable, depending on the key success factors defined for the specific organization.

Metrics

There are many sources of information on metrics (such as *Keeping Score* by Mark Graham Brown and *Four Practical Revolutions in Management* by Shoji Shiba and David Walden), each with its own perspective. The Baldrige Award requirements and the Balanced Scorecard views are presented for reference along with several other nonexhaustive lists that may help the thinking of groups searching for the right metrics. The key to developing the right metrics is to ensure that they align with the organization's objectives as defined in Chapter 8.

Baldrige Award Requirements

The core requirement categories for the Baldrige National Quality Award are listed below. Please note that the specific requirements vary by type of organization and can be updated yearly. (The following criteria are from the *2004 Criteria for Performance Excellence* booklet for business organizations published by the Baldrige National Quality Program and available online at www.quality.nist.gov.)

1. Leadership
2. Strategic planning
3. Customer and market focus
4. Measurement, analysis, and knowledge management
5. Human resource focus
6. Process management
7. Business results

The Balanced Scorecard View

The view put forward by the title *The Balanced Scorecard* by Robert S. Kaplan and David P. Norton is that metrics should be in balance among the four categories below:

Financial Perspective

- Return on investment/economic value add
- Profitability
- Revenue growth/mix
- Cost reduction productivity

Customer Perspective

- Market share
- Customer acquisition
- Customer retention
- Customer profitability
- Customer satisfaction

Internal Business Perspective

- Quality
- Response time
- Cost
- New product introduction

Learning and Growth Perspective

- Employee satisfaction
- Employee retention
- Employee productivity
- Information system availability

Sample Lean Business Metrics for a Total Enterprise

Financial

- Sales revenue
- Sales growth (market share)

- Return on net assets (RONA)
- Earnings before interest and taxes (EBIT), or earnings before interest, taxes, depreciation, and amortization (EBITDA)
- Cash flow

Customer

- Customer satisfaction
- Production launched 100 percent on time
- Commitments met 100 percent on time

People

- Employee satisfaction
- Training hours per person per year

Operations and Productivity

- Sales per engineer
- Value added per employee
- Improvement per year percent
- Production up-time percent

Quality

- Quality—ppm (parts per million defective){stretch goal of zero ppm}.

Technology

- Development time less than ____ months
- Number of patent applications

Sample Business Metrics

Customer

- On-time response
- Percentage of on-time delivery
- Overall satisfaction
- Percentage of retention
- Percentage of quotations accepted (business to business)
- Number of complaints (or complaints per million units shipped)
- Number of new customers per year (business to business)
- Number of new customer programs per year (business to business)

People

- Overall employee satisfaction
- Annual turnover
- Training hours per year
- Absenteeism
- Turnover
- Community satisfaction
- Person hours of company supported community service

Safety and Environmental

- Number of accidents
- Lost-time accidents
- OSHA recordable rate
- Percentage of environmental inspections passed
- Person hours of safety training per year

Productivity

- Projects per year
- Engineers per project
- $ per project
- # design drawings per designer per year
- Sales $ per person
- Sales $ per engineer
- Value added $ per employee
- Development cycle effectiveness = working development time (days)/development throughput time (days)

Financial

- Percent value-added [(value-added time/total time) × 100 percent]
- Sales
- Sales growth or market share
- Sales growth in nontraditional markets
- Return on net assets (RONA)
- Economic value added (EVA)
- Earnings before interest and taxes (EBIT)
- Return on equity
- Annual cost-reduction rate

Quality

- Defects per project
- Number of product changes
- Number of process changes
- Person hours of rework effort
- Cost of quality
- Supplier quality

Cost

- Number of cost overruns
- Percentage of projects delivered at or below cost targets
- Percentage of projects delivered at profit targets
- Percentage of budget attainment

Delivery

- Number of perfect production launches
- Number of late customer commitments
- Percentage of "clean" production launches at start of production
- Average days to fill order/request
- Quotations made within __ days
- Number of premium shipments
- Supplier delivery performance

Technology

- Number of new (successful) product launches
- Number of patent applications
- Percentage of sales from new products
- Percentage of sales from proprietary products
- Number of new product introductions versus competition
- Development cycle time and lead time
- New product revenue per engineer

And, of course, many others are possible. Select the metrics that will measure progress toward the objectives and drive the behaviors to accomplish the strategies.

Reference: Key Lean Manufacturing Metrics

- Delivery performance percent
- Customer returns (PPM)
- First time quality (FTQ) percent
- Scrap percent
- Process uptime percent
- Capacity utilization percent
- Total product cycle time (dock-to-dock)
- Total product cycle time improvement percent
- Inventory turns
- Process cost improvement percent
- Unit cost improvement percent
- Parts per labor-hour
- Injury rate
- Attendance rate
- Continuous improvement participation percent

Flow Analysis

The analysis of process flow is one of the key techniques in lean implementation. Please refer to the process analysis discussion in Chapter 9 for an overview and an example. The following section presents the basic concepts for flow analysis.

The Benefits of Flow Analysis

- Flow analysis provides a visual reference of process relationships:
  - Provides mechanism for all team members to become familiar with the process in a common language.
  - Provides reference for measurement of improvement.
  - Provides a consistent approach to process analysis.
    - Process flow
    - Controls and decision points
    - Communication system
- Flow analysis identifies opportunities for improvement:
  - Identifies the long lead-path through the value chain.
  - Identifies waste in the process.
  - Allows for optimization of the system to improve response to the customer.

General Approach

The general approach in flow analysis consists of six parts:

1. Current state documentation:
- Create the baseline for improvement.

2. Ideal state definition:
- Identify the ideal process (define perfection).
- This also creates an ongoing improvement target.

3. Desired state development:
- Develop the process that will be implemented as the improved design.
- Consider improvements that can be made in the near term:
  - Analyze non-value-added activities for opportunities to reduce, eliminate, or combine.
  - Analyze value-added activities for opportunities to reduce, eliminate, or combine.
  - Improve flow of material, people, and information.
  - Address causes of waste (waste is not the problem but a symptom).

4. Plan the implementation:
- Create detailed step-by-step plans to implement the improvement ideas.
- Consider potential problems and risks and address accordingly.

5. Manage the implementation:
- Monitor progress and collect feedback comments—adjust as necessary.

6. Continuous improvement:
- As progress is made, continue to consider how aspects of the ideal state can be applied into the desired state.

Flow Analysis—Process Flow Evaluation

Evaluate the flow of a process by charting the steps of the primary and feeder processes and documenting key data that describes the state of each step and its relative contribution to the value stream. The fundamental steps are as follows:

- Define the process boundaries clearly.
- Develop a visual representation of the process—Create an initial flowchart and document the facts regarding the process and its performance:
  - Establish the sequence and relationships of the process steps:
    - Check for missing or incomplete steps by walking through the process using the diagram.
  - Document specific detail and performance data within each process step using the process element data sheet in Figure D.1.
  - Analyze the process elements using the process element analysis worksheet shown in Figure D.2.
  - Consider process interactions using the relationship interaction analysis worksheet shown in Figure D.3.
- Understand the lead time and value through the entire process:
  - Identify the long lead path (critical path).
  - Identify the time required for the entire process.
  - Identify bottlenecks and buffer processes.
  - Identify communication problems.
- Be certain to evaluate people, material, and information flows.
- Include interaction with suppliers and customers (both internal and external).

This current state analysis establishes the foundation for generating improvement ideas. Use this same type of thinking process for completing the ideal state and the desired state. Then define the detailed implementation plan, obtain any approvals required, and begin making progress. When large numbers of analyses are going on simultaneously, some organizations define standard flow analysis symbols and charting standards to help ensure clear communication.

Flow Analysis Worksheets

In completing flow analysis (process analysis) activities, the worksheets in Figures D.1, D.2, and D.3 have proven very helpful. Having a structured approach to evaluating process elements and interactions is valuable in capturing key inputs. Completing these sheets for flow analysis projects will usually lead to an improved understanding and better improvement ideas.

Figure D.1 shows the process element data sheet. It is a generic data sheet to provoke thinking. One may need to add or delete items for particular applications.

Process Element Data Sheet

Process: _____ Date: _____

Process Information	Observations
Detailed description of what happens	
Number of people involved directly in the process	
Number of people supporting the process	
What data is regularly measured or collected?	
Method of information transfer	
Documents used	
Process time	
Wait time	
Identify if the process is value added (or what portions are)	
Tools or equipment used	
Special observations and issues (known problem areas, alternate processing, etc.)	

Figure D.1: Flow Analysis—Process Element Data Sheet

Figure D.2 shows the process element analysis worksheet that should be completed for each process element in the flow. The measures area is to capture any and all metrics used to evaluate the effectiveness of the process described.

Process Element Analysis Worksheet	
Process Name	List key interactions affecting the process or accomplishment of process objectives:
	•
Process Description	•
	•
	•
	•
Measures	Identify actions to improve the process:
	Actions *Who* *When*
•	•
•	•
•	•
•	•
	•

Figure D.2: Flow Analysis—Process Element Analysis Worksheet

Figure D.3 shows the relationship interaction analysis worksheet where the circle shows the relationship number from the flow analysis diagram and the performance area is a description of how the interaction is processed (completed).

Relationship Interaction Analysis Worksheet	
◯ **Interaction Name**	**Issues**
	List any issues that are affecting or impacting the relathionship:
Performance	•
•	•
•	•
•	**Actions**
•	Identify actions to improve the effectiveness of the interaction:
Measures	Actions Who When
•	•
•	•
•	•
•	•
	•

Figure D.3: Flow Analysis—Relationship Interaction Analysis Worksheet

Hints for Current State Flow Analysis

- Intent
  - Create a flowchart (map) of the process as it is actually done.
- Hints
  - Walk through the process:
    - Identify exceptions and norms.
    - Evaluate the flow from customer back to supplier:
      - Information

- Material
- People
- Process
- Observe feeder processes for wasteful activity.
- Watch for differences in actual processes used versus intended procedures (many times the actual process is a better way).
- Consider customer and supplier interactions.

Hints for Ideal State Flow Analysis

- Intent
  - Create a flowchart of the process without any waste.
  - Envision a perfect world.
- Hints
  - Avoid accepting current practices required by today's system design.
  - Watch for blocking paradigms.
  - Do not allow current organizational structures or facility layouts to limit possibility thinking.
  - Strive to allow only value-adding activities in the process.
  - Keep customer and business value added in focus.

Hints for Desired State Flow Analysis

- Intent
  - Create a flowchart of the process as we should strive to make it.
  - Reminder—this defines the next major level of improvement.
- Hints
  - Ensure stakeholder ownership of improvement design.
  - Design for no mistakes.
  - Focus on improving value-added flow:
    - Reduce
    - Eliminate
    - Combine
  - Design with stretch goals (or competitive benchmarks) in mind.
  - Non-value-added activity is allowed, but make sure to minimize.

Hints for Identifying and Exploiting Constraints

- Definition
  - Bottleneck process—an activity or process that impedes, and is the major restriction to, the process flow.
- Hints
  - Identify the steps where material, information, or people are delayed—waiting on processing (blocked or starved).
  - Optimize to ensure the bottleneck has maximum throughput:
    - Increase capacity of a bottleneck operation.
    - Improve process to reduce waiting time.
    - Assure the process has optimum up-time (support the bottleneck).
  - Consider the impact on the flow if a bottleneck process is used to pace the operation.

E

Implementation Formats

Action Plans

It is absolutely critical to track action plans and manage implementation. Action plans may be tracked individually using traditional methods, as shown in Figure E.1.

Item Number	Action	Due Date	Party Responsible	Strategy and Goal Coverage

Figure E.1: Traditional Action Item Tracking Format

Action plans may also be grouped into initiatives. An initiative may have metrics as well as action plans associated with it as is discussed in Chapter 10. A blank format is shown in Figure E.2.

Note: Organizations with a longer term focus may prefer to convert the schedule section into a monthly or weekly calendar with symbols to indicate planned and completed milestones.

Initiative: _____   **Strategy:** _____

Objective   **Value**   **Goal:** _____

Background

Accomplishments (since last update)

Action Plan

Item Description	Resp.	Due Date

Schedule (for overall initiative)

Milestone	Progress %	Date Complete	Target Date

Owner: _____   Created: _____

Updated: _____

Team members: _____

Support people (optional): _____

Figure E.2: Blank Strategic Initiative Format

Technique Selection: An Objective Approach

The following objective approach is offered as a proposed learning concept, not as a general process. It can be helpful in clarifying thinking, building understanding, or documenting the thinking of a decision process. It has been used very successfully to help sort between a limited few techniques in cultures driven by committee-style, logic-driven decision making. On a large scale, it can become very cumbersome, can be the source for endless debate over weighting and scoring, and may consume significant time. *Use carefully recognizing the risks mentioned.*

A technique selection analysis process follows, using the dual filter concept shown in Figure F.1. The two filters are current performance and targeting.

Current Performance Evaluation

- What is not working well and is causing big waste?
- How good, fast, and competitive (total performance) are we?
- How much do we need to improve?
- In the given situation and system, what techniques might make sense?

In the current performance filter, quality, lean flow, and speed were chosen as key issues to rate.

Targeting Evaluation (Value)

- How much will fixing it help us?
- Will we be successful?
- How important is it for the short term and for the long term?

In the targeting filter, benefit, ease to implement, and strategic value were chosen as key issues to rate.

Opportunity Targeting Process—Visualization

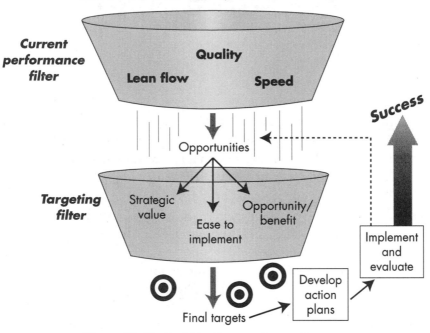

Figure F.1: The Dual Filter Targeting Process Concept

The steps for filling out the matrix in Figure F.2 are as follows:

1. Determine weighting factors and relationships for rating criteria:
- Should total 100 percent for each level (performance and targeting)
- Relative weights of each category should be balanced in relation to the entire business direction:
  - 10 - maximum, very important.
  - 1 - minimum, not important.

2. Identify techniques and/or applications to be rated from various sources.

3. Determine ratings for each proposed technique in each performance and targeting category:

Performance

- 10 - high level of competence with ongoing improvement.
- 5 - average level of competence compared to competition.
- 1 - little or no competence.

Targeting

- 10 - high level of opportunity or impact.
- 5 - moderate level of opportunity or impact.
- 1 - low level of opportunity or impact.

4. Calculate total weighted performance/targeting rating (scoring).

5. Evaluate in Pareto format for priority consideration.

6. *Decide* which activities or issues to improve.

One should consider the following rating hints when developing an objective analysis:

- Select values for the rating scales from a high-level perspective—think in the range of high (10) and low (1), not the difference between 4.1 and 4.7
- Only include detailed inputs and analysis to a level needed to identify the top areas to investigate in order to avoid analysis paralysis.
- Additional areas can be investigated using detailed analysis once the activities are in progress for the areas initially selected.

The dual filter process was shown in Figure F.1, an example results worksheet is shown in Figure F.2, and a Pareto of results is shown in Figure F.3.

As Figures F.2 and F.3 show, techniques 2 and 1 were chosen for the initial implementation based on the total weighted score, and then, six months later, techniques 9 and 5 were introduced.

Typically, this type of objective approach selects the same techniques as the intuitive approach. However, the dialogue created to generate the weightings and valuations can lead to a common understanding of the differing viewpoints. This understanding may result in improved alignment and commitment to implementation action.

Potential Techniques	Performance Ratings			Weighted Perf. Rating	Target Ratings			Total
	Quality	Lean flow	Speed		Oppor-tunity/ Benefit	East to Implement	Strategic value	Total Weighted Targeting Rating
Rating Category Weight Factor (%)	30%	40%	30%	10%	10%	20%	60%	100%
Technique 1	1	2	10	4.1	5	6	8	16.09
Technique 2	3	1	1	1.6	3	4	10	16.94
Technique 3	2	1	3	1.9	1	2	1	10.91
Technique 4	4	9	8	7.2	2	3	1	10.68
Technique 5	3	1	1	1.6	1	3	4	12.94
Technique 6	2	1	1	1.3	1	2	3	12.17
Technique 7	5	4	7	5.2	4	1	1	10.68
Technique 8	6	1	1	2.5	7	4	1	11.85
Technique 9	1	6	1	3	5	8	2	13.00
Technique 10	2	1	5	2.5	8	7	1	12.55

Figure F.2: Technique Selection Analysis—Example

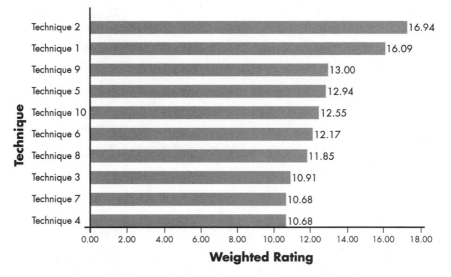

Figure F.3: Pareto Analysis of Potential Techniques—Example

Paradigm Discussion Processes

Paradigm discussions can be very interesting and usually require proactive facilitation. The following suggestions may be used in conjunction with the methods discussed in Chapter 12 to set the stage for the paradigm discussions.

Suggestion One: Define the pressures to change.

What pressures are creating the need for us to change?

- Customer/Market needs?
- Competitor actions?
- Organizational pressure (Needs)?

Suggestion Two: Define the future outlook.

What does our future look like on our current path?

- In 1 year?
- In 5 years?
- In 10 years?
- In 20 years?

Paradigm Worksheet

In completing the paradigm process worksheet of Figure G.1, the following potential categories of business paradigms may be helpful to stimulate the breadth of thinking required.

- Market
- Customers
- People
- Management/leadership
- Technology
- Products
- Quality
- Costs
- Pricing
- Competitors
- Business systems
- Service
- Financial
- Suppliers
- Manufacturing
- Development

Paradigm	Help or Harm	Requirements	Sustainable	Impact	Actions

Figure G.1: Paradigm Process Worksheet

SUGGESTED READING AND RESOURCES

Excellent "How To" Books

Jackson, Thomas, and Karen Jones. *Implementing a Lean Management System*. New York: Productivity Press, 1996.

Jackson, Thomas, and Constance Dyer. *Corporate Diagnosis*. New York: Productivity Press, 1996.

Haines, Stephen G. *The Systems Thinking Approach to Strategic Planning and Management*. Boca Raton, FL: Saint Lucie Press, 2000.

Shiba, Shoji and David Walden. *Four Practical Revolutions in Management—Systems for Creating Unique Organizational Capability*. New York: Productivity Press, 2001.

Excellent Books

Ackoff, Russell. *Creating the Corporate Future—Plan or Be Planned For.* Hoboken, NJ: John Wiley and Sons, 1981.

Kaplan, Rogert S., and David P. Norton. *The Balanced Scorecard*. Boston: Harvard Business School Press, 1996.

Brown, Mark Graham. *Keeping Score—Using the Right Metrics to Drive World-Class Performance*. New York: Productivity Press, 1996.

Ollhoff, Jim, and Michael Walcheski. *Stepping in Wholes—Introduction to Complex Systems*. Eden Prairie, MN: Sparrow Media Group, 2002.

Hammel, Gary, and C. K. Prahalad. *Competing for the Future*. Boston: Harvard Business School Press, 1994.

Delavigne, Kenneth T., J. Daniel Robertson, and Daniel Robertson. *Deming's Profound Changes—When Will the Sleeping Giant Awaken?* Englewood Cliffs, NJ: PTR Prentice Hall, 1994.

Kotter, John. *Leading Change*. Boston: Harvard Business School Press, 1996.

Maurer, Rick. *Beyond the Wall of Resistance—Unconventional Strategies that Build Support for Change*. Austin: Bard Books, 1996.

Rodgers,T.J., William Taylor, and Rick Foreman, *No Excuses Management*. New York: Currency-Doubleday, 1992.

Womack, James, and Daniel Jones. *Lean Thinking.* New York: Simon and Schuster, 1996.

LeBoeuf, Michael, Ph.D. *The Greatest Management Principle in the World.* New York: G.P. Putman's Sons, 1985.

De Pree, Max. *Leadership Is an Art.* New York: Bantam Doubleday Dell Publishing Group, 1989.

INDEX

ABOUT THE AUTHORS

The three authors are from Direction Associates, Inc.—a business strategy consulting firm specializing in helping organizations become more successful. They are experts in implementing the concepts that they have so graciously shared in this book, and have been successfully doing so since 1996.

George A. Shinkle, BSME, MBA, PE

Vice President of Direction Associates.

George combines 7 years of international consulting experiences with over 17 years of varied technical and management experiences gained while working for General Motors to provide a unique perspective on how to make organizations successful. He is recognized for his ability to provide support for strategic organizational alignment, lean management systems implementation, lean enterprise implementation, marketing strategy, program management, technology planning and implementation, and quality improvement. He has worked with customers worldwide, and understands the unique needs of American, European, African, and Asian customers.

George was trained by Toyota to appreciate and understand the concepts of lean. He is experienced in the Toyota Production System; has directed technical, manufacturing, and commercial groups worldwide; has developed successful new technology products; has been awarded patents; and was recognized with the prestigious Kettering Award. He managed a $600 million global business.

Lloyd H. "Reb" Gooding, BSME, MSIA, Numerous Advanced Study Programs

President and founder of Direction Associates.

Reb is an experienced international consultant and has worked with clients in the automotive industry, component manufacturing, the restaurant industry, the sport fishing industry, and not-for-profit charitable organizations. He couples his consulting experience with over 25 years of business experience at General Motors directing business segments, strategic planning, marketing, and sales groups. Reb's experience with organizations in Asia, Africa, Europe, Latin America, and North America provides a global perspective to his consulting. Reb is expert at directing senior management retreats, aiding middle management teams in becoming aligned, and in acting as a sounding board for individuals at all levels of the organization.

Reb's management experience in the automotive industry includes building a business from $10 million to $200 million in sales in four years in a high growth segment and managing a $500 million global business segment. This, combined with his international consulting background, provides a unique perspective on what organizations are facing today, and a basis from which to tailor unique lean processes for clients, which focus on understanding, asset alignment, implementation, and, ultimately, improved organizations. He is skilled at aiding clients to quickly identify and focus on key issues, to think into the future, see implications, and chart a course of appropriate actions.

Michael L. Smith, BSME

Direction Associates Consultant to the manufacturing and service industries.

Mike has over 15 years of experience in manufacturing, quality, process design, and product design at General Motors and Delphi Automotive. He has worked internationally as a consultant with diverse global customers for the past five years. He has lead projects in lean management systems, lean manufacturing, and QS9000 certification, and he has delivered significant results in these areas for his clients.

Mike is gifted with the ability to see how to improve the leanness of processes, which many others struggle to see. Having been trained in Toyota production methods, he is highly skilled in lean manufacturing methods and has fulfilled the role of lead "sensei" in many plant wide improvement projects. Mike draws on his depth of practical experience in directing plant-level improvement, product and process design, quality, lean implementations in engineering, and lean implementation in business systems, to clearly communicate the essence of how to successfully implement lean throughout the organization.